LETTERS @ WORK

READING and SPELLING

Volume 2: Book One
Consonants' Teams

Joel Morine

Illustrated by

Dana Clark

IMAGO
PRESS
TUCSON ARIZONA

Letters @ Work, Volume 2: Consonants' Teams

Copyright © 2003, 2007 by Joel Morine

Published in the United States of America by:

Imago Press
3710 East Edison
Tucson AZ 85716-2912

First Edition

Library of Congress Cataloging-in-Publication Data

Morine, Joel.
  Letters @ work : reading and spelling / Joel Morine ; illustrated by Dana Clark.—1st ed.
     p. cm.
  Includes bibliographical references and index.
  ISBN 0-9725303-1-2 (pbk. : alk. paper)
  1. Reading—Phonetic method. 2. Word recognition. I. Title: Letters at work. II. Clark, Dana, 1975- ill. III. Title.
  LB1573.3.M67 2003
  372.46'5—dc22

2003019443

Book and Cover Design by Leila Joiner
Illustrations by Dana Clark

Printed in the United States of America

ISBN 978-0-9725303-1-6
ISBN 0-9725303-1-2

To the many meanings of the word "family."

Acknowledgments

Letters @ Work is an homage to six educators.

The McGuffie Readers organize sensible juxtaposed contrasts of sounds' spellings, letters' sounds, and sentence constructions, offered in instructive stories with "common sense" themes.

Dr. Seuss is still the best reading teacher in sight for young readers, forty plus years after he made the switch from whimsically humorous adult art books to whimsically humorous, and instructive, children's art books. Other authors' pictures illustrate their words, whereas his words illustrate his pictures, which is what frees his stories for the styles of redundant spelling that he uses so effectively to train Readers. His real art is joyful learning, his sentences play bongos.

Both my parents, **Dr. Harold Morine and Dr. Greta Morine-Dershimer,** were teachers, authors and developers of teacher training programs.

Dr. Caleb Gattegno's math and language arts tools point out many possibilities of color as a mnemonic scaffolding tool. His Words In Color language arts program, in dozens of languages, addressed interesting, important process goals that most curriculums can't. Dr. Gattegno's Cuisenaire Rods, as employed by **Roland Genise**, taught me the values of the Jungle Gym instructional mode/metaphor/strategy.

Adopted from all of these six chosen models is a primary goal to improve a student's rate of knowledge acquisition by challenging, exercising and improving a student's focus on **how to learn!** These guiding lights offered well-organized data, time to ponder it, questions that prompted children to ask their own questions. They greeted errors cheerfully as the doors we learn through. Learn to learn, watch how you learn, have a purpose, look for ways to meet goals, try ideas and witness their effect, build or even invent your own tools. Enjoy it!

—**Joel Morine**

LETTERS @ WORK

READING and SPELLING

Volume 1: Letters' Sounds

Volume 2: Consonants' Teams

Volume 3: Vowels' Teams

A LearnerTools Product

Table of Contents
Volume 2, Book One: Consonants' Teams

Pages: Book One

PAGES: BOOK ONE (CONTINUED)

Pages: Book One (continued)

PAGES: BOOK TWO

PAGES: BOOK TWO (CONTINUED)

Pages: Book Two (continued)

INTRODUCTION

Spelling is TEAMwork by the Letters!

We, the Letters, wrote this book for you to learn how we spell, so you can read us and spell us!

Our book is organized for each letter to explain to you the work it does spelling.

Then you will practice reading the letter in words and sentences until you are good at that.

When you practice reading words, you will learn to spell some of those words, just by reading them.

The more you practice, the faster you will learn to read and spell with each new letter you meet.

We have tried to offer some ways to make your practice more fun and more helpful.

Each Chapter begins with some Practice Suggestions that you may want to try.

Each Chapter ends with two Games that the Reader and Learner can use to practice.

Your goal in each page is **learn to do what is practiced on that page!**

Any practice that gets you to that Goal is good practice for you!

Some activities you may want to come back to after several pages, or to skip entirely.

With some activity pages, you may prefer to read the answer page before you do the activity.

Do not feel you must do every activity the directions offer. You know you, we don't.

We hope future editions will carry an Appendix of other ideas for activities, thought of by you.

There is one other way to help yourself learn faster. **Learn to Learn!**

> Know what your goal is when you begin each practice!
>
> Think about your goal as you practice!
>
> Notice how that page's activity helps you reach that page's goals!

The more you learn about HOW TO LEARN, the faster and better you will learn!!!

There are two Scripts (or Fonts, if you prefer) used in this Volume.

The words "Font," or "Script," refer to the style and size of the letters.

There are small differences in shape and size from one font to another.

The sentences written with this Script are for the Reader (helper) to read to the Learner.

This Script is used for the letters to introduce themselves and to tell you about how they spell.

We suggest that the Learner point to each word, and read along when you can, as the Reader reads.

The words and sentences written with this Script are for the Learner to learn to read.

Each section of this Script should be read first by whoever the Learner chooses.

The Learner's goal is to learn to read all the words and sentences written with this Script.

The Learner's goal is also to learn to spell most of those words and sentences.

Any page that wasn't very easy to do the first time is a good page to do several times.

With the hardest pages, do the page several times in a row, one after another.

Most pages about any subject that is new to you are best done every day or two for a week.

Learning to spell is easier when you read more often.

When you read, you are also watching someone spell well.

Your brain is automatically remembering how to spell some of those well-spelled words.

It is easier to read than to spell, but reading often makes both spelling and reading easier to learn!

These books are not a complete language arts program, and are not intended to be.

This can be an effective piece of, or addition to, any in-school or home-school reading program!

Our goal here is to provide a fun, practical, effective practice tool for those who want to use one!

We cannot teach you, but we can help you

Learn To Learn...

PRACTICE CALENDARS

You may want to keep a record of your practice.
Each Chapter has a Practice Calendar.

Keeping a Practice Calendar will help some Learners practice more often, and longer.

Readers will want to help Learners learn, and remember, to fill in the Calendar, if they use one.
We call it a Practice Calendar, not a Practice Log, so Learners will think of it as a **daily** activity.

And, of course, you can practice without a Practice Calendar.

We do recommend having a Notebook for your spelling and writing practice.

Send us a copy of your Practice Calendar when you are finished...if you want to.
Your Practice Calendar may help us make our book better each year.
Only Learners and Readers like you can answer our favorite questions about our book and you:
> How old are you?
> For each page, each day:
>> Which ways did you practice the page?

>> Was the page FUN!!? Was the page fun? Was the page not fun?

>> Did you read the page quicker than the last time you read this page?

>>> Was the page hard or easy for you when you began?
>>> Was the page clear or confusing for you when you finished it?

>> Was your 1st time reading that page with NO errors the
>>> 1st, 2nd, 3rd, 4th, 5th, 6th time you read that page?
> Which pages did you learn to read each week? Which did you learn to spell?

If you wish to send us a copy of your practice calendar, the address is: LearnerTools
304 Lake Forest Lane
Charlottesville VA 22901

Comments can be e-mailed to: SpeakToMe@LearnerTools.net

How you practice our pages is entirely up to you to decide!

Use **ANY or NONE**

of our **directions and Practice Suggestions,**

or use **your own Practice Plan,**

or use **a Plan you use in school.**

Try lots of Plans.

Decide which Plans help you most.

Decide which Plans you enjoy most.

Think of this as a jungle gym!

YOU decide how to climb around in it!

What helps YOU when YOU try it?

That is your Plan for choosing your Practice Plans.

Notes

CHAPTER 1

Goals

Notice letters' sounds you already learned by hearing, reading and writing them in sentences.
(pp. 23 - 25)
Meet and practice (f v z j) and the teams (dge ge gi).
(pp. 26 - 42)
Meet and practice recognizing Nouns and Noun Families.
(pp. 27 - 30 , 34)
Meet and practice recognizing Verbs and Verb Families.
(pp. 27 - 28, 30 , 34 - 35)
Read Silent E ending in some words.
(pp. 27 - 29, 33 - 35 , 40)
Meet and practice A in AVE and I in IVE spelling two different sounds.
(pp. 27 - 29, 40)
Meet and practice O in OVE spelling 3 different sounds.
(pp. 28 - 29, 40)
Practice expecting what a missing word in a sentence will be from the sense of the sentence.
(pp. 29 , 36 , 38 - 39)
Practice colorizing some letters' sounds with our Sound Symbols.
(pp. 24 - 25 , 27 - 28 , 40)

Here are some Practice Suggestions you may want to try.

Pages can be read consecutively, one reading per page, as is normal when reading books.

Pages can also be used in any other order you choose to use them, or repeated as often as you like.

It may be better, when a page is hard the first time you read it, to read it again a 2nd and 3rd time.

For most learners, it will be best to read almost all the pages 3 to 5 times each, or more.

Do all writing lightly in pencil, so you can easily erase a page to write lightly on it a 2nd and 3rd time.

Time the seconds a Learner uses to read a page each time. Write the times in your Practice Calendar.

At the end of every 3 to 5 pages, re-read the previous 3 to 5 pages consecutively.

PRACTICE CALENDAR
CHAPTER 1

DAY & DATE	TIME	PAGE	NOTES, COMMENTS

If you read all of Volume 1, by now you have learned to read many letters and their sounds.

You have practiced reading and spelling many letters who introduced the sound they spell to you.

You have even learned to read some sounds of letters and teams that did not introduce themselves.

The Words Lists below begin with words we used in our "Which make sense?" pages in Volume 1.

Have you learned to read some of these words while you read the "Which make sense?" pages?

Lightly, with a pencil, write a check by the words you can read in the Words Lists below.

we	we	they	they	my	you	all
he	was	day	the	by	do	ball
she	what	Thursday	then	try	to	tall
me	when	Saturday	them	fly	too	small
be	went	Sunday	this			wall
bee	will	today	that	of		
see	were	play	with	from	said	your

Can you read the sentences below?

They play all day every Thursday, Saturday and Sunday, and they are playing today.

They play many ways when they play all day.

"Try to Fly" is the way that they play to begin the day when they play all day.

"Try to Fly" is the way they play to end the day when they play all day.

They also play other ways than "Try to Fly" on the days they play all day.

When they play all day they get to play all the ways they can play.

They play all the ways they all can play, then play other ways, then play "Try to Fly."

Will you feel bad if you play all day? Will you feel bad if you see me play all day?

If you see I can play all day, and you can play all day, too, then will you play with me?

When we get to play all day, we play so long that then we can't remember what we played.

Try to use your Vowel Sound Symbol Tools to colorize the Words Lists below.

Use page 187 to pick the right pencil or marker and the symbol. Use page 189 to correct your work.

First colorize A's Name Sound in every word below where you hear A's Name Sound.

Now do the same for E, I, O, and U's Name Sounds, wherever you hear them in the words below.

Next colorize each of the 5 vowels' Short Sounds, one vowel sound at a time.

Finally, colorize the schwa sound wherever you hear it as you read yourself the words below.

we	we	they	they	my	you	all	say
he	was	day	the	by	do	ball	says
she	what	today	then	try	to	tall	saying
me	when	stay	than	fly	too	small	said
be	went	play	this	dry	two	wall	
bee	will	players	that	sky	of		
see	were	ways	with		from	your	or

pump	sing	see	sink	think	bring	buy	sit
pumps	sings	sees	sinks	thinks	brings	buys	sits
pumping	singing	seeing	sinking	thinking	bringing	buying	sitting
pumped	sang	saw	sank	thought	brought	bought	sat

fast	big	small	thin	thick	lower	slow
faster	bigger	smaller	thinner	thicker	lower	slower
fastest	biggest	smallest	thinnest	thickest	lowest	slowest

Is the schwa sound (the "quick, quiet sound") a vowel sound?   Yes, the schwa is a vowel sound.

Did some of the words have two vowel sounds in the same word?   Can you underline those words?

How many words from the lists above can you underline in the sentences on the next page?

They play ball on Saturday, on the thick grass of a soccer field.

The smaller soccer players seem to run and turn faster than most of the taller players do.

We play handball all day every day, hitting the small ball against the tall wall.

They play soccer Thursdays and Saturdays, if they see that the sky is dry.

We saw that singer singing in a play last Saturday, a play with a lot of singing.

We sat on the small wall under the tall hill thinking of ways to play and stay dry.

We had to play inside today, to stay dry, all day long.

I underlined   _____   words from page 24.

You can use page 189 to check your choice of which words to underline.

Below, use the first two words from each sentence above to help you think of sentences you can write.

You can use them as a start to your sentences, or write your own beginnings.

Use as many of the words from page 24 as you can while writing your own sentences or story.

Write your sentences (or story if you prefer) in your own notebook.

They play

The smaller

We play

They play

We saw

We sat

We had

For each sentence you wrote, write the number of words from page 24 that you used in that sentence.

Can you colorize the vowel sounds in the words you underlined? In the sentences you wrote?

Use the directions at the top of page 24 to colorize whichever you choose.

How do you do? I am F. I am pleased to meet you.

Fiddle

I am easy to read. I always spell the same sound!

Well, almost always.

I am a little bit harder to spell.

I am not the only Letter who can spell my sound.

In Chapter 11, H will tell you how H helps spell my sound in two of H's teams, GH and PH .

I am only in one team, in a very few words. E will tell you in Chapter 11 about the team I am in.

You will want to practice reading me as I spell my F sound.

fix	flux	fin	fins	flip	frill	fig
fox	flex	fun	fund	flop	frog	fog
fax	flax	fan	fans	flap	frost	fad
fixes	flexes	fen	fender	flag	fret	fed
foxes	flecks	font	fonts	flab	Fred	full

These 4 important words you may have already learned to read by reading them in "sense" sentences.

for   from   front   of

Of all the words on this page, in which one word do I not spell my F sound?

Here are two hints.

One, the sound I spell in that word is the sound V spells.   (See next page for the sound V spells.)

Two, the word begins one sentence on this page.

Look at and say the first word in each sentence to find the word.

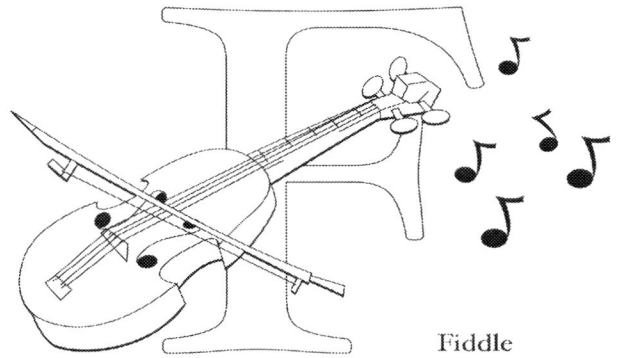

I am V. I am so easy to read that I will not even say how to read me.

You will know as soon as your Reader reads these Words Lists to you!

van	vim	vans	vigor	valor
vat	vent	vents	venting	vast
Val	vend	Val's	vendor	Victor

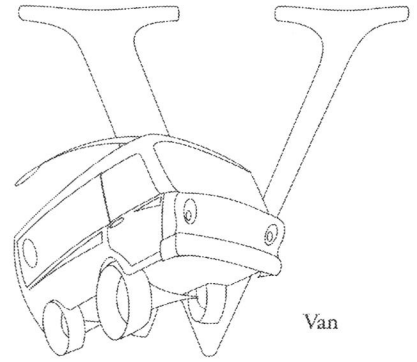

Van

I am easy to spell, too. You already know the only time another letter spells my sound.   of

I spell my sound alone when at the start or in the middle of a root word.   river canvas oven

When my sound is the last sound in a word, I spell my sound, but I am never the last letter of a word.

When my V sound is the last sound in a word, a silent E always follows me to finish the word.

Listen as your Reader reads below. How many sounds does I spell in the Words Lists below?

How many different sounds does A spell in the Words Lists below?

Can you spell some of these words in your Notebook as your Reader reads them to you?

give	live	life	wife	hive	dive
gives	lives	lives	wives	hives	dives
giving	living	gift	jive	diver	diving
gave	lived	gifts		divers	dove

have	half	calf	brave	pave	save
has	halves	calves	braves	paves	saves
having			braving	paving	saving
had			braved	paved	saved

Use this page to check your spelling, then colorize just Name Sounds and Short Sounds of I and A.

Use pg. 187 to choose tools and symbols. Use pg. 190 to check your colorizing when you are done.

give	live		dive	strive	drive
gives	lives		dives	strives	drives
giving	living		diving	striving	driving
gave	lived		dove	strove	drove

How many different sounds does I spell in front of VE in the Words Lists above?   _____

How many different sounds does O spell in front of VE in the Words Lists below?   _____

love	glove	cover	oven	above		stove	clove	clover
loves	gloves	covers	ovens			stoves	cloves	clovers
loving	gloving		glove	dove			drove	cove
loved	gloved		gloves	doves			droves	coves

move	move	remove	prove	disprove	approve	improve
moves	moves	removes	proves	disproves	approves	improves
diver	driver	moving	removing	proving	disproving	approving	improving
divers	drivers	moved	removed	proved	disproved	approved	improved

The many sounds O spells in OVE is the only thing hard about reading me, V !

Practice reading the words above in the sentences below.

Can you colorize them in the sentences below?

Use page 187 to choose your tools. Use page 190 to check your choices of symbols and colors.

We strove to move clover from the grove over the river, to move the clover by the cloves.

We put our gloves on, put the clover on trucks, and the drivers drove the trucks.

The drivers drove the trucks full of clover over the river, where we removed the clover.

We had our gloves on to remove the clover from the trucks that drove it over the river.

We removed the clover from the backs of the trucks that drove the clover over the river.

As we put the clover in stacks by the cloves, our stacks improved, they got a bit better.

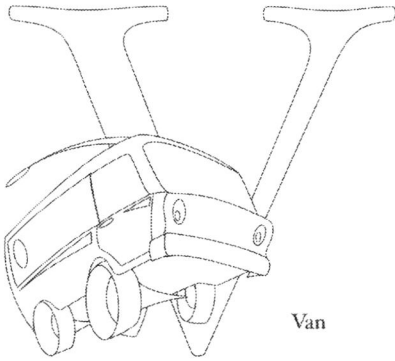

In the words below, another letter follows the E that follows me, V.

given	seven	eleven	oven	gravel	level
givens	sevens	elevens	ovens	gravels	levels
driver	river	cover	favor	mover	lever
drivers	rivers	covers	favors	movers	levers

Van

The E near the end of all the above root words except "favor" is spelling the _____ sound.

I have a liver. She has a liver. He has a liver. You have a liver. We all have livers in us.

Can you give a river a gift? Can a river give you a gift?
If I give a gift to you and you give a gift to me, you will have given and gotten a gift.
If I give a gift to you and you give a gift to me, I will have given and gotten a gift, too.
Two of us will have given one gift and gotten one gift, but two gifts will have been given.

As a favor, I drove seven ovens and four stoves, in my truck, over the river to Grover's.
Seven ovens plus four stoves was eleven heavy things to lift on and off the truck.
Driving the truck with eleven heavy things is not extra difficult, the truck is strong.

The dove is called the bird of love, but all birds love the birds they love.

We drive across six rivers when we drive to Riverville. There are four we do not cross.
Our drivers drive on nine different bridges when crossing six rivers in Riverville.
Why is Riverville called "Riverville"? Riverville has ten r_____ by it.

How did you choose a word to fill the blank at the end of the last story? That is called "context."
You can blank 1 word in any paragraph of any story to practice using context to get clues as you read.

The E near the end of the words that end with ER, EL or EN is spelling the schwa sound.

The next section of Words Lists are Noun Families. Nouns are words for <u>places</u>, <u>creatures</u> or <u>things</u>.

The first, shortest word in every Word Family is called the Root Word.

The Root Word in a Noun Family is the word for saying ONE of that place, creature or thing.

The second word in a Noun Family almost always ends with S.

A Noun Family's S-ending word means MORE THAN ONE of that place, creature or thing.

You will practice recognizing and using Nouns and Noun Families in Chapters 3 and 4.

fox	fender	liver	font	vat	raft	van
foxes	fenders	livers	fonts	vats	rafts	vans
frog	vendor	river	vest	van	bird	lap
frogs	vendors	rivers	vests	vans	birds	laps
dove	oven	frill	factor	sax	frog	ring
doves	ovens	frills	factors	saxes	frogs	rings
glove	cover	gift	vent	flipper	flip	thing
gloves	covers	gifts	vents	flippers	flips	things

The Words Lists below are Verb Families. Verbs are words for <u>actions</u>, words for <u>doings</u> or <u>activities</u>.

The first word in our Verb Family lists is always the family's Root Word.

You will practice recognizing and using Verbs and Verb Families in Chapter 2.

give	cover	flip	flop	flatter	filter	fling
gives	covers	flips	flops	flatters	filters	flings
giving	covering	flipping	flopping	flattering	filtering	flinging
gave	covered	flipped	flopped	flattered	filtered	flung

Gil *gives* back the toy I *gave* to him when I ask him to *give* it to me. Gil likes *giving*.

Hi. I am Z!

I am pleased to meet you!

I don't do much! Really, I don't.

But I'm not lazy. Really, I'm not.

Did you ever notice how S ends so many words?

You see, S really likes to spell my Z sound to end Nouns and Verbs.   So I let S.

is	has	spells	Sam's	balls	bugs	fins
was	walls	fills	pumps	pens	figs	fingers

When S ends a word, it seems like S almost always spells my Z sound.

Sometimes when S ends a word, S spells the S sound.

You will know when, when you read the word and say it and recognize it. Your tongue will tell you.

tips	clicks	pits	cliffs
stops	clocks	pets	surfs

You can practice reading me in these words.

zig	jazz	drizzle	Zen	drizzles	fizzes
zag	fizz	fizzle	fez	fizzles	buzzes
zip	buzz	dazzle	Liz	dazzles	jazzes
zap	fuzz	nozzle	sizzle	sizzles	razzes

Spelling isn't my only work!

I also work in the comics page of the newspapers.

They use me to show that the characters in a comic are sleeping or snoring.   "Zzzzzzzzzzzzz."

Which make sense?

Which do not?

Frogs have seven fins in them and eleven livers on them.

Foxes have no fins on them and one liver in them.

> Foxes are strong drummers from lots of drumming.

> Frogs are strong jumpers from lots of jumping.

It drizzled from six to eleven this morning.

The sun drizzled and the river sizzled from six to twelve the next morning.

> The pan was so hot the food in it fizzled.

> The pan was so hot the food in it sizzled.

It seldom drizzles in the desert.

The dessert is a long list of drizzling, wet riddles.

> We went to the vet in a van, the cat, my mom and I.

> We went to the vet, my cat and I, in my dog's van.

When a dog nuzzles its puppy, is it kissing the puppy?

When a dog nuzzles its puppy, it is selling the puppy.

> Six singers sang sixty wet, sandy, drizzling songs.

> Seventy singers sang seven long, funny songs.

"The snack I prefer is plump, tender duck," said the fox, with a dazzling grin.

A fox can not tell you with words what the fox wants for a snack.

> Two, four and six are even numbers.

> Seven is not an odd number.

Eleventy sixty less seventy is forty.

Eleven less seven is four.

> Seven plus seven is seventy-seventeen.

> Seven plus seven adds up to fourteen.

I'm J. Who are you?

Just like F and X and Z, I almost always spell the same sound.

| jug | jam | Janet | job | jump | jingle |
| jig | jog | Jimmy | jot | jumble | jungle |

Just like F and X and Z, I am not the only Letter to spell my sound.

G can team with E or I or Y to spell my sound. Y will show you examples of the GY team later.

When my J sound ends a word, I never spell it, ever.

To end a word with my J sound, E teams up with G, and the E will spell silence.

urge	bulge	judge	edge	badge	trudge
surge	singe	budge	ledge	pledge	ridge
merge	lunge	fudge	dredge	lodge	bridge

D says some people don't hear a D sound if it is followed by GE spelling the J sound, and some do.

Sometimes the GE team does not end the word. Then E spells the sounds E usually spells.

| gem | gender | gel | gentle | gentleman | germ | gerbil |
| | urgent | indulgent | | emergent | tangent | badger |

In these next words, the GI team spells my J sound. Does I also spell a sound in these words?

| gist | magic | tragic | magical | urging | merging | lodging |
| giblet | rigid | logic | margin | surging | verging | dodging |

In a GI team, I spells the sounds I usually spells, but G spells my J sound.

Many words are Root Words in both a Noun Family and a Verb Family.

The Noun and Verb sound the same and are spelled the same, but their meanings and uses differ.

<u>Noun Families</u>

jog	judge	lodge	pledge	giggle	tingle	bag
jogs	judges	lodges	pledges	giggles	tingles	bags
jogger		lodger		giggler		bagger
joggers		lodgers		gigglers		baggers

<u>Verb Families</u>

jog	judge	lodge	pledge	giggle	tingle	bag
jogs	judges	lodges	pledges	giggles	tingles	bags
jogging	judging	lodging	pledging	giggling	tingling	bagging
jogged	judged	lodged	pledged	giggled	tingled	bagged

Each Noun Family in the top row above looks the same as the first 2 words in the Verb Family below it.

The Root Word and the S-ending word have the same spelling, and sound the same.

When you use Root Words or S-ending words in sentences, you use them as a Noun or as a Verb.

You use them as a Noun when they refer to the thing, or place, or creature.
You use them as a Verb when they refer to the action.

Using "jog" as a Noun: I will go for a jog. Then I will go for a second jog.
Using "jog" as a Verb: I jog fast at first. Then I jog less fast as we jog longer.

In the sentences below, the <u>Nouns</u> are <u>underlined</u>. The *Verbs* are in *italics*.

The <u>judge</u> is at the <u>lodge</u> to *judge* <u>fudge</u>. The <u>judge</u> *judges* <u>fudge</u> better than <u>lodgers</u> *do*.
The <u>judge</u> *pledged* to *judge* the <u>fudge</u> perfectly. The <u>judge</u> *jogged* to the <u>lodge</u> yesterday.
The <u>judge</u> is *lodging* at the <u>lodge</u> until he *judges* all the <u>fudge</u> the <u>lodgers</u> need *judged*.

Each of these stories practices 1, 2 or 3 Verb Families. The *Verbs* of those Verb Families are in *italics*.

There are other Verbs used in the stories also. The other Verbs are <u>underlined</u>.

The judge *judges* the other joggers when he *jogs*, and *judges* the jugglers, too.

The other joggers don't <u>like</u> the judge to <u>be</u> *judging* their *jogging*.

The jugglers don't <u>like</u> the judge to <u>be</u> *judging* their *juggling*.

In the judgment of the joggers and jugglers, the judge <u>is</u> just too judgmental.

There <u>is</u> some justice to the joggers and jugglers *judging* the judge to <u>be</u> too judgmental.

The judge *judges* the joggers and jugglers to <u>be</u> too judgmental towards the judge.

The gentle little badger *snuggled* with her mommy, and her sisters and brothers.

The mommy badger *snuggling* with her little badgers <u>was</u> happy.

Badgers can <u>be</u> gentle when they *snuggle* with the rest of the family.

The daddy badger *snuggles* with all the other badgers in his family.

She *gives* gifts. He *gives* gifts. They *give* gifts. We *give* gifts. I *give* gifts.

She *gave* a gift Saturday. He *gave* a gift Sunday. They *gave* gifts Saturday and Sunday.

Dad *gives* gifts every Monday. I *give* gifts every Monday, too.

Dad *gave* a gift last Monday. I *gave* a gift this past Thursday. We *gave* gifts last week.

Dad <u>will</u> *give* a gift next Monday. I <u>will</u> *give* a gift next Thursday.

She <u>will</u> *give* a gift next Saturday. He <u>will</u> *give* a gift on Sunday. We all <u>have</u> gifts to *give*.

I <u>had</u> the urge to *trudge* up the hill. I <u>had</u> the urge to *trudge* down the hill.

I <u>had</u> the two urges to *trudge* up and down the hill. It <u>added</u> up to one long trudge.

I <u>felt</u> an urge to *run*. I <u>felt</u> a surge of energy in my legs. I just *ran* up the hill.

I <u>felt</u> a surge of energy in my legs, and <u>wanted</u> to *run*, so I *ran* up the hill. It was a fun run.

Jimmy can *juggle*. Jimmy can *jog*. Jimmy can *judge* fudge.

Jimmy can *juggle* and *jog* and *judge* fudge; but Jimmy can not <u>do</u> them all together.

Can you use the first line of each story to tell you how to fill in the blanks in the second line?

Will asked me to be a judge. The judging is Saturday at the lodge.

Will asked me to be a judge Saturday at _____ _____ .

We eat fudge. We have the fudge in a box. The box is by the edge of the hedge.

We eat the fudge we have in the box by _____ _____ of the hedge.

Mom and Dad trim the top of the hedge. They cut it with hedge cutters.

Mom and Dad _____ the top of the _____ with hedge cutters.

Jennifer has a hamster.   Jennifer has a gerbil. Jennifer has a grasshopper in her garden.

Jennifer has a _____ and a _____ and a grasshopper in ____ _____ .

Jill has fudge. Her fudge is in a box. The box is in her fridge.

Jill has a _____ of _____ in her fridge.

Jeff loves to eat fudge. Jeff loves to eat berry jam. Jeff loves to play in the sand.

Jeff _____ to eat fudge and berry jam and to play in the _____ .

I can spell "fudge." I can spell "judge." I can spell "trudge."

I ____ _____ "fudge" and "judge" and "trudge."

Jessica can giggle. Jessica can juggle. Jessica can tangle and untangle string.

Jessica _____ giggle and juggle and Jessica _____ also tangle and untangle string.

Jimmy is jogging. Jimmy was jogging yesterday. Jimmy will jog Saturday.

Jimmy ___ _____ and _____ _____ and _____ ____ this week.

The bottom line in each pair combines all the sentences in the top line.

Sometimes, when E or I follow G, they are not a team, E or I are just next to G.

get	give	gills	giving	geld
getting	given	Gilbert	gifts	gild

Letters spell as a team to help each other spell different sounds than they spell alone.

How do you know if they are being a team or not when they are right next to each other?

Try saying the word both ways, as if they were a team, and as if they were not a team.

Which of the two ways makes sense as a word? Does the word make sense in the sentence?

Can you still recognize the ways my J sound is spelled when all the ways are mixed together?

You may want to start by underlining GE and GI wherever you see them below.

Remember, when GE ends a word, G always spells my J sound.

Other times you see GE or GI, try the G sound and the J sound, and decide which one makes sense.

When GE or GI begin a word, G often spells the G sound, and often spells the J sound.

jam	badge	singe	gist	badge
jelly	jig	job	edge	badger
jump	Janet	juggle	dredging	gel
gem	judge	gentle	trudge	get
surge	bulge	ledge	trudging	give
logic	bulging	jingle	jot	engine
jig	urge	jiggle	jungle	singe
gift	urging	fudge	Jack	ridge
gills	verge	tragic	Jeff	bridge
magic	verging	giggle	gender	juggling

Try reading those Words Lists again after you've practiced the next 3 pages as many times as you like.

Can you use the sense of the sentences, and your memory of the story, to spell the missing words?

Read a story 3 times, then cover it with a piece of paper and try to spell its missing words in the copy.

The juggler was juggling jugs of jelly and glass jars of purple jam.

The joggers were jogging past the juggler, dodging the jugs that the juggler dropped.

The judge of the fudge contest sat across from the juggler as the joggers passed by.

"My fudge is the best fudge ever," said the judge, "but I can't be in the contest."

The joggers and the juggler all giggled at the judge after the judge said that.

The biggest jogger was wiggling his fingers as he giggled at the judge's comments.

The judge asked the juggler to juggle the joggers. Do you think the judge was kidding?

The juggler was _____ jugs of jelly and glass jars of purple jam.

The joggers _____ jogging past the juggler, dodging the jugs that the juggler dropped.

The judge of the fudge contest sat across from the juggler as the joggers passed by.

"My fudge is the best fudge ever," said the _____ , "but I can't be in the contest."

The joggers and the juggler all giggled at the judge after the _____ said that.

The biggest jogger was wiggling his fingers as he giggled at _____ judge's comments.

The judge asked the _____ to juggle the joggers. The judge giggled as he asked.

Is it a struggle for you to jump rope for a hundred jumps with no stop?

I struggled to jump a hundred jumps of jump rope last month, but I jumped them today.

If I jump every day this month, then next month I expect I'll be stronger than this month.

My record is one hundred and twenty seven jumps with the jump rope with no stopping.

I jump rope well. Jumping rope is fun.

Is it a struggle for you to jump rope for a hundred jumps with no stop?

I struggled to jump a hundred jumps of _____ rope last month, but I jumped them today.

If I jump every day this month, then next month I expect I'll be stronger than this _____.

My record is one hundred and twenty seven _____ with the jump rope with no stopping.

I _____ rope well. _____ rope is fun.

Continue using the same directions you used for the last page.

I live with my mom by the edge of a park. My dad lives by a different edge of the park.

My mom and I walk across the park to get to my dad's when I stay with my dad.

My dad and I walk across the park to get to my mom's when I go back to my mom's.

Mom's apartment is my home. Dad's apartment is my home, too. I have two homes.

Both my homes are by the park. Mom and Dad play different games with me in the park.

It is hard to have two different homes, but it is fun to have two different homes, too.

I live with my mom by the edge of a park. My dad lives by a different edge of the _____.

My mom and I walk across the park to get to _____ dad's when I stay _____ my dad.

My dad and I walk _____ the park to get to my mom's when I go back to my mom's.

Mom's apartment is my home. Dad's apartment is my home, too. I have two _____.

Both my homes are by the park. Mom and Dad play different games with ____ in the park.

It is hard to have two different homes, but it ____ fun to have _____ different homes, too.

I was asked to be a Jam Judge. I was glad. I love blackberry jam.

I love every berry jam. My sister loves berry jams, too.

The person that asked me to be a Jam Judge, told me the judging is Saturday at the lodge.

I expected the lodge to be filled with jam cooks and Jam Judges and jam fans. And bread.

I got to the judging at the lodge on Saturday, but I didn't smell or see any bread or jam.

Then they began to play music using lots of different instruments. A music jam?!

I was asked to be a Jam Judge. I was glad. I love blackberry jam.

___ love every berry jam. My sister _____ berry jams, too.

The person that asked me to be a _____ Judge told me the judging is Saturday at the lodge.

I expected the lodge to be full of jam cooks and Jam Judges and jam fans. And bread.

I got to the judging at the _____ on Saturday, but I didn't smell or see any bread or jam.

Then they began to play music using lots of different instruments. A music _____ ?!

Words in the lists below use sounds, spellings, and patterns you practiced reading in this chapter.

First, colorize A's Name Sound wherever you hear it below, then E, I, O and U's Name Sounds also.

Then colorize each of the 5 vowels' Short Sounds, and the schwa sound. Colorize 1 sound at a time.

No words below have U's Name Sound.

Colorize the sound O spells in "move" or "do" wherever you hear it.

drizzle	jog	germs	gist	judge
jazz	jam	gentle	magic	lodge
guzzle	jump	urgent	urging	pledge
fizzes	just	gender	gym	giggle
zen	jingle	gerbil	energy	tingle

fix	self	life	van	give	gave
fizz	surf	safe	vigor	live	have
fall	sniff	strife	ever	strive	save
flex	sniffles	sofa	never	drive	wave
fins	soft	wife	serve	dive	paved

move	love	seven	driver
remove	gloves	eleven	river
prove	oven	given	liver
disprove	cover	gravel	favor
approve	over	level	flavor
improve	stove	pivot	lever

move	love	drive	give	have	see	say	do
moves	loves	drives	gives	has	sees	says	does
moving	loving	driving	giving	having	seeing	saying	doing
moved	loved	drove	gave	had	saw	said	did

You can check your work on page 191.

Jenny loves fudge, so she cooks it for the judge; but she won't eat any fudge!

The judge eats fudge, dripping with grape jelly, just as he gets to his gym each day. He jumps jumping jacks and joins joggers to jog with them, and then he juggles jars of berry jam. Judge James "Jimmy" Johnson just joined his gym, for jumping jacks and jogging and juggling. The judge drives to the gym every day; just after he has fudge.

Jenny loves to cook fudge for the judge. How would Jenny feel if she knew that the judge always ate her special fudge dripping with grape jelly? How would you feel?

When the judge eats her fudge, he does not really eat it at first. At first, the judge licks the fudge. Then, second, the judge nibbles the fudge. Then he eats chunks of fudge.

When the judge licks the fudge, at first, the fudge is not yet dripping with jelly. The judge does not add the jelly until the judge is done nibbling the fudge. When the judge is ready to eat chunks of fudge, then the judge adds the jelly, grape jelly.

Then, just like Tony the Tiger, the judge yells, "Grape jelly is Great!"

"Grape jelly on great fudge is great!" roars the judge, like a fantasy tiger who talks.

The judge also likes to juggle, and to travel in the jungle.

The judge likes to travel in the jungle, watching the animals, eating fudge that is dripping with great gobs of purple grape jelly, yelling, "Grape jelly is Great!" back at the lions and tigers, whenever the lions and tigers roar at the judge first.

"Don't be silly, dear!" says the judge's wife, when the judge roars, "Grape jelly is Great!", just like Tony the Tiger, at the lions and tigers.

"Great!" the judge roars at his wife, when his wife tells the judge, "Don't be silly, dear!" The judge roars it just like Tony the Tiger does when the judge roars "Great!" to his wife, too. Have your ever roared, "Great!", like a fantasy tiger? Is it fun?

The judge only roars at his wife like that when the judge and his wife are in the jungle. The judge loves his wife, and the jungle too. The judge's wife loves to hear the judge roar when she is with him in the jungle. They like to roar together, "Great!"

Were any words in this story hard to read? Did the sense of the sentence help you read them?

Reading sentences is not like reading lists. The sense of the sentence helps you read some words.

You have already read, in practice sentences, words with letters or letter teams we hadn't told you.

Try to read these sentences by using the math you know to help you figure out the new number words.

All these stories add up to ten. You have ten fingers. Your fingers can help you add.

When <u>two</u> edgers edge grass and <u>eight</u> edgers edge glass, that is <u>ten</u> edgers edging things.

When <u>seven</u> lodgers lodge in cabins and <u>three</u> lodgers lodge in tents, that is <u>ten</u> lodgers.
<u>Seven</u> lodgers plus <u>three</u> is <u>ten</u> lodgers lodging in cabins or tents.
<u>Ten</u> lodgers lodging in cabins or tents, plus <u>two</u> lodgers lodging in the lodge, is <u>twelve</u>.
<u>Seven</u> lodgers in cabins, <u>three</u> lodgers in tents, <u>two</u> lodgers in the lodge, is <u>twelve</u> lodgers.
Isn't it? Will <u>seven</u> plus <u>three</u> plus <u>two</u> add up to <u>twelve</u>, or is it <u>eleven</u>? Can you say?

<u>Six</u> judges judging in court and <u>four</u> judges judging in offices is <u>ten</u> judges judging.

When <u>one</u> badger lodges in a hedge and <u>nine</u> badgers lodge in holes, that is <u>ten</u> badgers.

When <u>nine</u> edgers edge hedges every Saturday and <u>one</u> edger edges hedges every Sunday,
                    that is <u>ten</u> edgers edging hedges every weekend. <u>Nine</u> plus <u>one</u> is <u>ten</u>.

When <u>five</u> dodgers dodge dodge-balls on <u>one</u> team,
        and <u>five</u> dodgers dodge dodge-balls on the other <u>one</u> team,
        and <u>one</u> dodger tells the story of <u>ten</u> dodgers dodging dodge-balls on the <u>two</u> teams,
that is a dodge-ball dodgers math story, "<u>Five</u> plus <u>five</u> is <u>ten</u> plus <u>one</u> is <u>eleven</u> dodgers."

<u>Ten</u> pins standing minus <u>zero</u> pins falling is <u>ten</u> pins standing. <u>Ten</u> minus <u>zero</u> is <u>ten</u>.
<u>Zero</u> fallen pins plus <u>ten</u> standing pins is <u>ten</u> pins in all. <u>Zero</u> pins plus <u>ten</u> is <u>ten</u> pins.
Roll the ball a <u>second</u> time and hit the <u>ten</u> pins with your <u>second</u> ball. Some pins will fall.
<u>Seven</u> pins standing. <u>Ten</u> pins in all, minus <u>seven</u> left standing, is <u>three</u> fallen pins.

Can you colorize the vowels of the words for numbers we underlined on this page?
Where can you check your work?

We call this "Authoring Math Stories."

An Author is the person who creates a story or a book or a magazine article.

The Author decides what the story will say, and then tells the story by writing it down.

You and your Reader will be co-authors, co-authoring the stories you write together.

Write your own 3 or 4 or 5 sentence math stories.   (L = Learner, R = Reader)

Take turns. First L tells a story and R writes it. Then R tells a story and L writes it.

Start the story with a list of simple sentences like the sentences in the top lines of the stories below.

The list of simple sentences should have similar sentences about similar actions or things.

Make the 2nd line a summing up sentence, that sums up both the actions and the number of things.

Then on the third line, write a sentence with just the math.

Author your story so that as many words as possible are words that you can spell yourself.

Here are 3 sample stories.

I have six red socks. I have six black socks. All my socks are dusty and dirty.
Six dusty, dirty red socks and six dusty, dirty black socks is twelve dusty and dirty socks.
Six plus six is twelve.

This nest has two birds. That nest has two birds. The other nest has six birds.
The three nests have two birds, two birds and six birds, for a total of ten birds.
Two plus two is four, plus six is ten.

Two clocks say one o'clock. Five clocks say five o'clock.   It is seven o'clock.
Two incorrect clocks and five incorrect clocks is seven clocks not telling the correct time.
Two plus five is seven.

On a left-hand page of your Notebook, list the words "one" to "ten" in one list.

On the same page, list the words "eleven" to "twenty" in a second list.

On the facing right-hand page, write your math stories.

That is "Authoring Math Stories."

We call this   **Illustrating Sentences.**

Pick 2 or 3 sentences from this chapter that you can draw.

<u>Underline</u> the sentences as you pick them.

Copy one of the sentences onto one of the blank spaces in the next few pages.

Draw a picture of the sentence above, below, or next to your sentence.

Copy the other sentences you <u>picked</u>, then draw pictures of them.

Write some sentences of your own for you to draw.

Use pencils and markers that are not colorizing tools to color the pictures of sentences you draw.

Then, if you want to, you can colorize your sentences. Page 187 lists our colorizing tools.

Colorize one or two vowel sounds at a time, in your sentences, using one or two colorizing tools.

After you colorize all the vowels that spell those 1 or 2 sounds, pick a different sound or 2 to colorize.

That is   **Illustrating Sentences.**

Celebrate finishing Chapter 1 by reading any or all of the following books.

The Name Jar   Yangsook Choi
Once Upon a Time   Niki Daly
Once Upon a Time   Vivian French, John Prater
Inside, Outside, Upside Down   Barenstain, Stan and Jan
The Cat in the Hat Beginner Book Dictionary   Dr. Seuss & P. D. Eastman

You can color these letters you have learned.

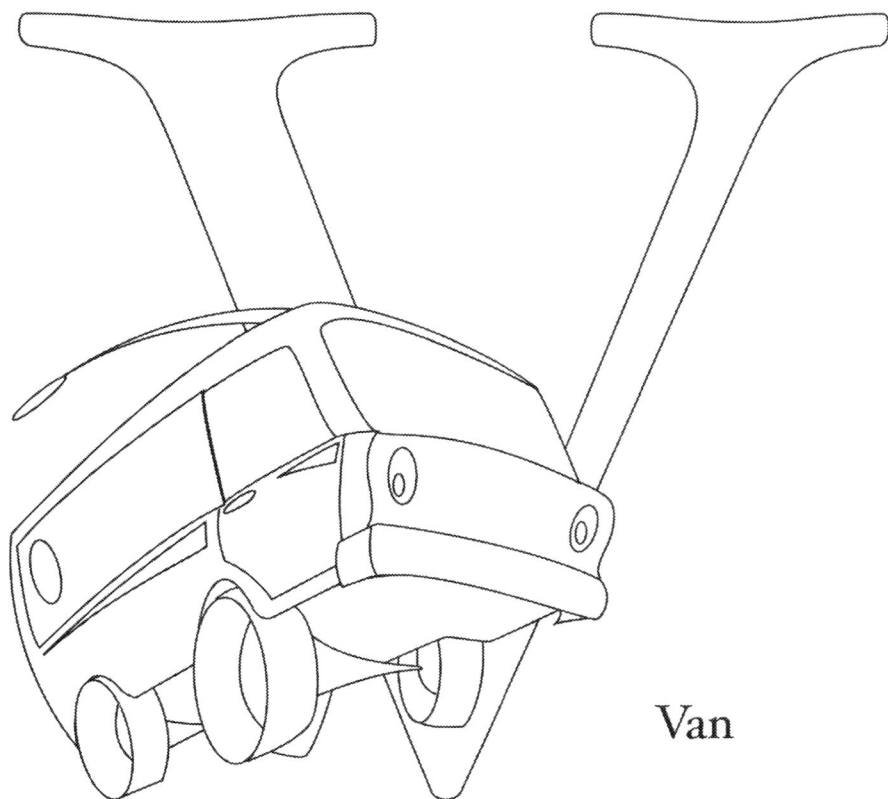

Van

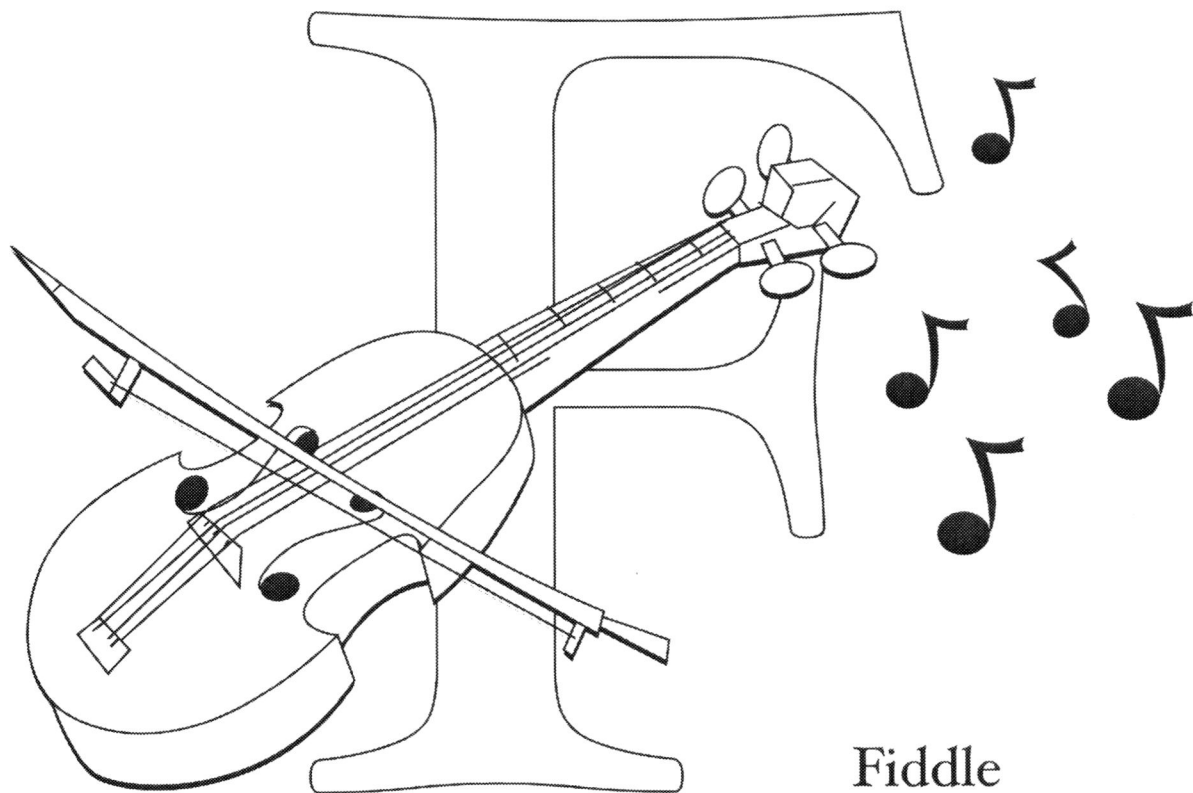

Fiddle

CHAPTER 2

Goals

Practice reading consonants you know how to read if you have read Volume 1.
  (p d t n s m l b c k r g x)   (pp. 49 - 65)
Practice recognizing Nouns and Verbs as you read sentences and Verb Family lists.
  (pp. 49 – 64 , 66)
Begin a habit of seeing words as members of a Family, who all share the same root word.
  (pp. 49 – 66)
Notice that Verb Family Lists have several different spelling patterns.
  (pp. 50 – 64 , 66)
Practice spelling patterns for Verb Families.
  (pp. 50 – 64 , 66)
Begin to think about when to use which member of a Verb Family when reading sentences.
  (pp. 53 , 55 , 57 , 59 , 61 , 65 - 66)

Here are some Practice Suggestions you may want to try.

Practice saying the words in the Words Lists in sentences, using each word in its own sentence.

Can you tell your Reader (or write in your Notebook) one short story that uses all the words in one list?
Use all the words in a Words List to tell or write your short story. Then put another list in another story.
Or take turns (with your Reader or a friend) each adding sentences to a story, using 1 or 2 Words Lists.
How many Words Lists can you fit into one story, using some of the words from each list?

Another suggested Practice Plan is to pick a Verb Family that is spelled "by the plan."
(You will learn what "by the plan" means as you read this Chapter.)
Copy the Root Verb of that Verb Family into your Notebook. Next, study the rest of that Verb Family.
Now, beneath the Root Verb, write the other 3 Verbs in the Verb Family you studied.
Then check your work.

PRACTICE CALENDAR
CHAPTER 2

DAY & DATE	TIME	PAGE	NOTES, COMMENTS

Do you know yet which Words Families are Noun Families and which are Verb Families?

You may want to re-read pages 30, 34 and 35 for extra practice before you read this page.

gift	flipper	jog	river	dove	girl	giraffe
gifts	flippers	jogs	rivers	doves	girls	giraffes

cover	oven	glove	vest	frog	finger	germ
covers	ovens	gloves	vests	frogs	fingers	germs

The two-word Word Families above are either Noun Families or Verb Families.

The four-word Word Families below are either Noun Families or Verb Families.

Which are the Noun Families and which are the Verb Families?

cover	flip	juggle	budge	tickle	give	have
covers	flips	juggles	budges	tickles	gives	has
covering	flipping	juggling	budging	tickling	giving	having
covered	flipped	juggled	budged	tickled	gave	had

When you see a whole family together, you can tell if it is a Noun Family or a Verb Family.

Many Root Words or S-ending words have a meaning as a Noun and a meaning as a Verb.

If you write those words, they don't have meaning until you use them as a Noun or use them as a Verb.

Until they are used in a sentence as a Noun or a Verb, they do not say which meaning they mean.

You practiced reading some words like that at the bottom of page 34.

For each word on the left, pick which sentence uses the word as a Verb, meaning an <u>action</u> or <u>activity</u>.

cover	Put the <u>cover</u> on the pot on the stove.	Can you <u>cover</u> the pot on the stove?
flips	My brother <u>flips</u> me over.	My sister can do back <u>flips</u>.
stick	I stuck a <u>stick</u> in the sand.	I will <u>stick</u> a pen in the sand next to it.
trip	Do not <u>trip</u> on those sticks.	We will go on a long <u>trip</u> this summer.
step	Can you <u>step</u> over that puddle.	I sat on the bottom <u>step</u> to rest.

Chapter 2 practices seeing and using Verbs and Verb Families.

Read us as we spell Verb Families for a page.

Verb Families use different spelling plans. All the Verb Families on this page are using the same plan.

This is the spelling plan for Verb Families whose Root Word ends with 2 consonants.

As you read each Verb Family, ask yourself:

What stays the same in all the words in a family?

What changes from word to word in these families?

back	track	snack	lock	block	clock	rock
backs	tracks	snacks	locks	blocks	clocks	rocks
backing	tracking	snacking	locking	blocking	clocking	rocking
backed	tracked	snacked	locked	blocked	clocked	rocked

pick	kick	trick	stick	tuck	lick	click
picks	kicks	tricks	sticks	tucks	licks	clicks
picking	kicking	tricking	sticking	tucking	licking	clicking
picked	kicked	tricked	stuck	tucked	licked	clicked

end	mend	blend	romp	print	plant	hand
ends	mends	blends	romps	prints	plants	hands
ending	mending	blending	romping	printing	planting	handing
ended	mended	blended	romped	printed	planted	handed

pluck	duck	dunk	drink	clink	clank	stink
plucks	ducks	dunks	drinks	clinks	clanks	stinks
plucking	ducking	dunking	drinking	clinking	clanking	stinking
plucked	ducked	dunked	drank	clinked	clanked	stunk

Which 3 Verb Families on this page have one word that is not spelled "by the plan" for these families?

Page 50 had Verb Families spelling the plan for Root Verbs that end with two consonants.

Here are two more pages of Verb Families spelling the same plan.

On pg. 50 we underlined some letters in each Verb Family, the same letters in each family (except 3).

Do you know how we chose the letters we chose to underline?

test	nest	rest	bang	sing	ring	sting	hang	bring
test<u>s</u>	nest<u>s</u>	rest<u>s</u>	bang<u>s</u>	sing<u>s</u>	ring<u>s</u>	sting<u>s</u>	hang<u>s</u>	bring<u>s</u>
test<u>ing</u>	nest<u>ing</u>	rest<u>ing</u>	bang<u>ing</u>	sing<u>ing</u>	ring<u>ing</u>	sting<u>ing</u>	hanging	bringing
test<u>ed</u>	nest<u>ed</u>	rest<u>ed</u>	bang<u>ed</u>					

Which two Verb Families would end with "singed" and "ringed" if their families spelled "by the plan?"

What word do you say or write instead of "singed?" What word do you say or write instead of "ringed?"

What words do you say instead of "stinged" or "hanged?" What word do you say instead of "bringed?"

We know you cannot spell the word people say and write instead of "bringed." It is   br<u>ought</u>

Can you spell the words you say instead of saying "singed," "ringed," "stinged," and "hanged?"

Write the last Verb in the last 5 families above, the 4th Verb for the Root Verbs.

                                                       sing   ring   sting   hang   bring

After you write the words, you can check your spelling when you get to the bottom of this page.

Below are more Verb Families that spell by the same plan, for Root Verbs that end with 2 consonants.

Can you underline the 3 endings that are added to the Root Verb in each list?

You can check your work on page 52.

stall	call	fall	spill	fill	spell	smell	sell	mull	pull
stalls	calls	falls	spills	fills	spells	smells	sells	mulls	pulls
stalling	calling	falling	spilling	filling	spelling	smelling	selling	mulling	pulling
stalled	called	fell	spilled	filled	spelled	smelled	sold	mulled	pulled

Is this how you spelled the missing Verbs?   s<u>a</u>ng   r<u>a</u>ng   st<u>u</u>ng   h<u>u</u>ng   br<u>ought</u>

Can you read all the words in these Verb Families?

test	nest	rest	bang	sing	ring	sting	hang	bring
tests	nests	rests	bangs	sings	rings	stings	hangs	brings
testing	nesting	resting	banging	singing	ringing	stinging	hanging	bringing
tested	nested	rested	banged	sang	rang	stung	hung	brought

stall	call	fall	spill	fill	spell	smell	sell	mull	pull
stall<u>s</u>	call<u>s</u>	fall<u>s</u>	spill<u>s</u>	fill<u>s</u>	spell<u>s</u>	smell<u>s</u>	sell<u>s</u>	mull<u>s</u>	pull<u>s</u>
stall<u>ing</u>	call<u>ing</u>	fall<u>ing</u>	spill<u>ing</u>	fill<u>ing</u>	spell<u>ing</u>	smell<u>ing</u>	sell<u>ing</u>	mull<u>ing</u>	pull<u>ing</u>
stall<u>ed</u>	call<u>ed</u>	f<u>e</u>ll	spill<u>ed</u>	fill<u>ed</u>	spell<u>ed</u>	smell<u>ed</u>	s<u>old</u>	mull<u>ed</u>	pull<u>ed</u>

What word do you say or write instead of "singed"?   _____

What word do you say or write instead of "ringed"?   _____

What word do you say or write instead of "stinged"?   _____

What word do you say or write instead of "hanged"?   _____

What word do you say or write instead of "bringed"?   _____

What word do you say or write instead of "falled"?   _____

What word do you say or write instead of "selled"?   _____

Do all of the Verb Families below spell "by the plan?"

pass	kiss	miss	boss	toss	fuss	muss	mess	cross
passes	kisses	misses	bosses	tosses	fusses	musses	messes	crosses
passing	kissing	missing	bossing	tossing	fussing	mussing	messing	crossing
passed	kissed	missed	bossed	tossed	fussed	mussed	messed	crossed

What extra letter was added to which verb-ending above? What sound did the extra E spell?

Can you guess why a schwa sound is needed after a Root Verb's SS, before its S ending?

E's schwa separates the S ending's sound from the root verb's SS, so you hear both S sounds.

Without E between SS and S, "passes" would be "passs" and sound just like "pass."

When you write, how do you choose which of the 4 Verbs to use when you need to use a Verb?

Here is a tool you can use, when you practice writing sentences, to choose a Verb.

I sink. You sink. We sink. They sink. My mom and dad sink.

Many dogs sink. Those kids sink. Rocks sink.

I _____.   You _____. We _____.   They _____.   He and she _____.

Many things _____.   Jill and Jack _____.

He sinks. She sinks. My mom sinks. My dad sinks.

One cat sinks. That kid sinks. A rock sinks.

He _____.   She _____.

One thing _____.   Jack _____.   Jill _____.

I am sinking. You are sinking. That kid is sinking. Those kids are sinking.

I like sinking. I hate sinking. I am good at sinking. I was sinking. I will be sinking.

I could be sinking. I would be sinking. I should be sinking. I have been sinking.

I am _____. She is _____. He is _____. We are _____. They are _____.

I was _____. She was _____. He was _____. We were _____. They were _____.

I like _____. She hates _____. We love _____. They are afraid of _____.

I will be _____. I could be _____. I may never be _____. I vote for _____.

Yesterday I sank. Last week she sank. Last month those kids sank. We all sank.

Yesterday I _____, he _____, she _____, we _____, you _____ and they _____.

Yesterday a dog _____. Yesterday many cats _____.

Last week everyone _____. Last month nobody _____.

Pick any Verb Family from any other page.

Use the Verb Family's 4 words correctly in the blanks above.

You can also add other words after the verb if you want to make longer sentences.

In each of the next 3 pairs of pages, the 1ˢᵗ page is filled with Verb Families that spell by 1 same plan.

The 2ⁿᵈ page is sample sentences using the 4 Verb Forms of some of the Verbs on the 1ˢᵗ page.

Each pair of pages lists Verb Families spelling by a different plan than the other two pairs of pages.

This pair of pages practices family spelling.

Is that the plan you just practiced on pages 50 – 52?   Yes.

While you practice Verbs in these pages, use your brain to picture a line under each Verb ending.

stamp	clamp	cramp	jump	dump	pump	limp	romp
stamps	clamps	cramps	jumps	dumps	pumps	limps	romps
stamping	clamping	cramping	jumping	dumping	pumping	limping	romping
stamped	clamped	cramped	jumped	dumped	pumped	limped	romped

stand	hand	band	brand	end	mend	bend	send
stands	hands	bands	brands	ends	mends	bends	sends
standing	handing	banding	branding	ending	mending	bending	sending
stood	handed	banded	branded	ended	mended	bent	sent

melt	tend	invest	bunt	punt	rant	grasp	rust	add
melts	tends	invests	bunts	punts	rants	grasps	rusts	adds
melting	tending	investing	bunting	punting	ranting	grasping	rusting	adding
melted	tended	invested	bunted	punted	ranted	grasped	rusted	added

jazz	fizz	buzz	miss	hiss	fuss	pass	sass	gas
jazzes	fizzes	buzzes	misses	hisses	fusses	passes	sasses	gasses
jazzing	fizzing	buzzing	missing	hissing	fussing	passing	sassing	gassing
jazzed	fizzed	buzzed	missed	hissed	fussed	passed	sassed	gassed

E in the ES-ending separates a Z or S sound ending a Root Word from the Z sound of the S-ending.

The E in an ES ending adds a schwa (Vol. 1, pg. 96) between 2 similar sounds, so you hear both.

Without E's schwa, "jazz" and "jazzs" would sound alike; so would "fizz" and "fizzs."

We call these **Verb Family Stories,** stories of 3 to 6 sentences that use all 4 Verbs in any Verb Family.

Bees *buzz* as they fly. One bee *buzzes.* Bees are *buzzing* now. Bees *buzzed* yesterday.

I *jump* up. My sister *jumps* off the steps. We like *jumping.* We *jumped* all day.

Sometimes my legs *cramp*, or one leg *cramps.* It hurts when they are *cramping.*
My legs *cramped* after my last long run in the hills.

I *pump* my tire as my sister *pumps* her tires. We are *pumping* with different pumps.
I just stopped *pumping* but I am not done. I *pumped* my tire too full!

I *bunt* a baseball better than my dad *bunts* a baseball. We still practice *bunting* together.
I *bunted* very well every week this month.

Do kittens *hiss*? Some kittens *hiss.* Does my kitten *hiss*? My kitten *hisses.*
My kitten is *hissing* now at a dog. Yesterday it *hissed* four times at my biggest dog.

With my red and purple ink stamp set, I *stamp* pictures onto all my letters.
My mom *stamps* pictures on all her letters, too, using my ink stamp set and my stamps.
My dad is *stamping* purple pictures of cattle with my cattle stamp now.
He likes *stamping* pictures of red and purple cattle on letters.
He *stamped* green cattle, too, until I ran out of green ink for my stamp pad.

I *invest* my time in learning. Focusing *invests* my time better than not focusing does.
I am *investing* my time every time I practice, so I focus when I practice, to *invest* it better.
I *invested* my time practicing for fifty minutes every day last week. I practiced spelling.

I *add* numbers fast with no pencil. I use fives and tens. For instance, I *add* nine fast.
Adding nine *adds* ten and subtracts one. Five plus ten is fifteen, minus one is fourteen.
Seven plus ten is seventeen, minus one is sixteen. Seven plus nine is sixteen.
Six plus ten is sixteen, minus one is fifteen. Six plus nine is fifteen.

When the Root Verb in a Verb Family ends with a single consonant following a Short Vowel Sound,

then that Verb Family spells by a different plan.

How does the spelling plan for the Verb Families on this page differ from the families on page 54?

trap	hop	stop	drip	step	snap	pad	drop
trap<u>s</u>	hop<u>s</u>	stop<u>s</u>	drip<u>s</u>	step<u>s</u>	snap<u>s</u>	pad<u>s</u>	drop<u>s</u>
trap<u>ping</u>	hop<u>ping</u>	stop<u>ping</u>	drip<u>ping</u>	step<u>ping</u>	snap<u>ping</u>	pad<u>ding</u>	drop<u>ping</u>
trap<u>ped</u>	hop<u>ped</u>	stop<u>ped</u>	drip<u>ped</u>	step<u>ped</u>	snap<u>ped</u>	pad<u>ded</u>	drop<u>ped</u>

strum	hum	drum	drag	plug	hug	tug	peg
strums	hums	drums	drags	plugs	hugs	tugs	pegs
strumming	humming	drumming	dragging	plugging	hugging	tugging	pegging
strummed	hummed	drummed	dragged	plugged	hugged	tugged	pegged

trim	slam	grab	fan	sled	pit	net	pet
trims	slams	grabs	fans	sleds	pits	nets	pets
trimming	slamming	grabbing	fanning	sledding	pitting	netting	petting
trimmed	slammed	grabbed	fanned	sledded	pitted	netted	petted

gab	bob	rob	lob	sob	pop	lap	tap	tip
gabs	bobs	robs	lobs	sobs	pops	laps	taps	tips
gabbing	bobbing	robbing	lobbing	sobbing	popping	lapping	tapping	tipping
gabbed	bobbed	robbed	lobbed	sobbed	popped	lapped	tapped	tipped

Which verb in each verb family below does not spell "by the plan?"

fit	sit	hit	spit	let	get	set	put	cut	run
fits	sits	hits	spits	lets	gets	sets	puts	cuts	runs
fitting	sitting	hitting	spitting	letting	getting	setting	putting	cutting	running
fit	sat	hit	spat	let	got	set	put	cut	ran

The Past Verb.

First, re-read just the *italicized* Verbs on page 55. Study how we <u>underlined</u> the endings of the Verbs.

For each italicized *Verb* below, <u>underline</u> all the letters that were *add<u>ed</u>* to that Verb Family's Root Verb.

I blow bubbles. I blow bubbles of bubble gum, and I blow bubbles from bubble suds.

When I blow bubbles of bubble gum, I *pop* the bubbles. My mom *pop<u>s</u>* bubbles, too.

We love *pop<u>ping</u>* the bubble suds bubbles with our fingers. It makes us both giggle.

Yesterday I *pop<u>ped</u>* bubbles of bubble gum, but not with my fingers, with a pin.

When I *pop<u>ped</u>* the bubble gum, it stuck to my lips. I had to get my lips unstuck.

My cat thinks I can *pet* her every minute of every day. Cats always expect us to *pet* them.

My cat never *pets* anyone. Have you ever seen any cat *petting* any animal ever?

I have asked my cat, whenever I *petted* my cat, for many years, to *pet* me back. Does it?

The fastest runner is going to *lap* the slowest runner. She *laps* a runner or two every lap.

She is way faster than all the other runners. She will be *lapping* six runners this lap.

She has never been *lapped* by any runner. She has never been passed by any other runner.

That is what proves she is the fastest runner, that no other runner has ever passed her.

She *lapped* twelve runners today. That is her personal record for most runners *lapped*.

My sister loves to *run*. I *run* too. She *runs* faster than I do. We like *running* fast.

We *ran* yesterday and today, and are going to *run* tomorrow, too.

I can *hit* a baseball well. My sister *hits* baseballs well, also. We both *hit* well.

We both like *hitting* baseballs to our parents. Our parents throw to us and we *hit* to them.

Hitting baseballs is fun. We *hit* baseballs every day last week after dinner.

I *cut* vegetables for dinner. My brother *cuts* vegetables with me every evening.

We have gotten better at *cutting* vegetables fast now that we practice every dinnertime.

We *cut* the vegetables for every dinner our family ate last month.

With which verb ending did you <u>not</u> need to repeat the final consonant: the S, ING or ED ending?

When the Root Verb in a Verb Family ends with an E, then that Verb Family spells by a different plan.

Study the Verb Families on this page. This spelling plan does something special to spell ING endings.

What do these Verb Families do differently than other families when spelling words with ING endings?

tremble	fumble	ramble	grumble	bundle	handle	scramble
trembles	fumbles	rambles	grumbles	bundles	handles	scrambles
trembling	fumbling	rambling	grumbling	bundling	handling	scrambling
trembled	fumbled	rambled	grumbled	bundled	handled	scrambled

bubble	juggle	fiddle	paddle	saddle	peddle	sizzle
bubbles	juggles	fiddles	paddles	saddles	peddles	sizzles
bubbling	juggling	fiddling	paddling	saddling	peddling	sizzling
bubbled	juggled	fiddled	paddled	saddled	peddled	sizzled

rinse	nurse	sense	pulse	move	live	give
rinses	nurses	senses	pulses	moves	lives	gives
rinsing	nursing	sensing	pulsing	moving	living	giving
rinsed	nursed	sensed	pulsed	moved	lived	gave

urge	merge	sponge	singe	lunge	drives	love	have
urges	merges	sponges	singes	lunges	drives	loves	has
urging	merging	sponging	singeing	lunging	driving	loving	having
urged	merged	sponged	singed	lunged	drove	loved	had

nudge	judge	budge	lodge	edge	pledge	bridge
nudges	judges	budges	lodges	edges	pledges	bridges
nudging	judging	budging	lodging	edging	pledging	bridging
nudged	judged	budged	lodged	edged	pledged	bridged

Which Verb Family above has 2 Verbs that do not spell "by the plan?"   have

Which 2 other Verb Families have Past Verbs that do not spell "by the plan?"   give   drive

Lightly with a pencil, <u>underline</u> any Verb endings we added to the Root Verb of that story's Verb Family. We did the first story for you. Can you <u>underline</u> the endings of the *italicized* Verbs in the 2nd story?

When a pot of water over a flame on the stove gets very hot, the water begins to *bubble*.

As the bubbling water gets hotter, it *bubbles* faster, until it *bubbles* over the top of the pot.

The hot water *bubbling* over the top of the pot can burn your hands if you handle the pot.

Handling a pot of hot water as it is *bubbling* over the top is not a happy thing to do.

If Jim *fumbles*, some fans *begin* to *grumble*.

If a fan *grumbles* to Jim, Jim *begins* to *grumble*.

If a lot of fans *grumble*, Jim *grumbles* a lot.

Jim does not like to *grumble*. Jim does not like to *fumble*.

The fans do not like Jim to *fumble*. But some fans do like to *grumble*. Some fans do not.

Jim likes to *handle* the football perfectly every time he gets the football.

Jim is *beginning* to get better at not *fumbling* the football, so the fans are *grumbling* less.

Last month, when Jim was *fumbling* a lot, the fans *grumbled* a lot.

But then Jim *began* to get better at *handling* the football. He *began* to *fumble* less.

Jim can be our best fullback if he *fumbles* the football less often.

Janet tells me Jim *fumbled* the basketball last spring during a dribbling contest.

The basketball contest fans *grumbled* a bit then, in the spring.

Janet is *grumbling* today as she tells me Jim *fumbled* a basketball last spring.

I'm *beginning* to get tired of Janet and other fans *grumbling* at Jim's *fumbling*.

I'm Jim. The fans and I *begin* to *grumble* whenever I *fumble*.

Can you spell the complete Verb Family for each of these Verb Roots?

Can you use all 4 verbs in each family in sentences? Can you use all 4 verbs in one story?

begin	handle	bubble	fumble	grumble
_____	_____	_____	_____	_____
_____	_____	_____	_____	_____
_____	_____	_____	_____	_____

Page 54 had Verb Families whose Root Verb ends with 2 consonants.

ask	rest	lick	hand	jump	toss	fizz
asks	rests	licks	hands	jumps	tosses	fizzes
asking	resting	licking	handing	jumping	tossing	fizzing
asked	rested	licked	handed	jumped	tossed	fizzed

Page 56 had Verb Families whose Root Verb ends with 1 consonant after 1 prior vowel's Short Sound.

strum	skip	grab	grin	stir
strums	skips	grabs	grins	stirs
strumming	skipping	grabbing	grinning	stirring
strummed	skipped	grabbed	grinned	stirred

Page 58 had Verb Families whose Root Verb ends with the letter E.

crinkle	rinse	lunge	mumble	move	glove
crinkles	rinses	lunges	mumbles	moves	gloves
crinkling	rinsing	lunging	mumbling	moving	gloving
crinkled	rinsed	lunged	mumbled	moved	gloved

Next to each Verb Family below, write which page number you would put that family on.

flop	nibble	mock	long	sag	rinse	nudge
flops	nibbles	mocks	longs	sags	rinses	nudges
flopping	nibbling	mocking	longing	sagging	rinsing	nudging
flopped	nibbled	mocked	longed	sagged	rinsed	nudged

Can you finish these Verb Families? Decide which plan a family uses, study the plan, then add 2 words.

nurse	sip	tap	struggle	nest	drum	list
nurses	sips	taps	struggles	nests	drums	lists

Use these Verb Family Stories to check your spelling of their families at the bottom of page 60.

I cut my hand yesterday while I was *drumming*. I cut it so bad I had to go to the hospital.

Doctors and nurses are the best at *nursing* you until you get better.

I can not *drum* until my hand is all better, it still hurts a little bit. I will *nurse* it longer.

Long ago, I cut my hand and *nursed* it for a whole month. I did no *drumming* for a month.

After that, when my hand was all better, I *drummed* every day for the next month.

If a drummer has the urge to *drum*, the drummer *drums* every day the drummer can *drum*.

Drumming every day gives a drummer the urge to *drum* every day the drummer can *drum*.

Some birds are *nesting* in our yard. Lots of birds *nested* in our yard last year.

Birds *nest* in our yard every year, but they only *nest* there in summer, not in the winter.

Not a single bird *nests* in our yard all winter long. Many a bird *nests* here in the summer.

I am *sipping* a glass of milk that is so good it is a *struggle* to just *sip* it.

It is so good I feel an urge to drink it fast, but I keep *struggling* to just keep *sipping* it.

Any person *struggles* to just *sip* any drink that is so good you want to drink it as one gulp.

My brother *sips* the milk as if he never *struggles*, but he is just pretending not to *struggle*.

My brother *struggles* to just *sip* good milk, too, even if he pretends he is not *struggling*.

I make lists. I *listed* my best books. I *list* all the letters at dinner every day.

I *list* all the numbers I can *list* whenever I take a bath.

My brother *lists* all the numbers he can *list* when he takes a bath, too.

This morning I am *listing* the verbs I can spell correctly. There are too many to *list*.

I can *drum* by *tapping* my pencil on my desk. After all, *drumming* is just *tapping*.

Sometimes when I *tap*, it bothers someone, so I *drum* by *tapping* my fingers on my leg.

My sister *drums* by *tapping* the fingers of her two hands together, *drumming* her fingers.

Do you have a way that you *drum* when you want to *drum* without bothering anyone?

I *drummed* my drum until it bothered someone, then I just *tapped* my leg.

Which families spell by the Verb Family Plan on page 54, for Root Verbs that end with 2 consonants?

Which families spell by the Verb Family Plan on page 56, for Root Verbs that end with 1 consonant?

Which families spell by the Verb Family Plan on page 58, for Root Verbs that end with the letter E?

Write the number "54," "56" or "58" lightly in pencil next to each Verb Family below.

When you are done you can check your answers using the next page.

snap	thank	drop	buckle	merge	belong	scoff
snaps	thanks	drops	buckles	merges	belongs	scoffs
snapping	thanking	dropping	buckling	merging	belonging	scoffing
snapped	thanked	dropped	buckled	merged	belonged	scoffed
scribble	nod	rub	bump	bang	plunge	rinse
scribbles	nods	rubs	bumps	bangs	plunges	rinses
scribbling	nodding	rubbing	bumping	banging	plunging	rinsing
scribbled	nodded	rubbed	bumped	banged	plunged	rinsed
cluck	step	stun	blink	crumble	rip	emerge
clucks	steps	stuns	blinks	crumbles	rips	emerges
clucking	stepping	stunning	blinking	crumbling	ripping	emerging
clucked	stepped	stunned	blinked	crumbled	ripped	emerged

First, find each family above on the next page. Compare your page number for each plan.

In the Verb Families using the plan from page 54, how is the Root Verb different from its ING verb?

In the Verb Families using the plan from page 56, how is the Root Verb different from its ING verb?

In the Verb Families using the plan from page 58 how is the Root Verb different from its ING verb?

Is page 60 or page 62 a better page to study to answer those 3 questions? Compare them to decide.

Now that you have studied each plan's spelling of ING words, can you spell the ING words below?

Afterwards, use page 62 to check and correct your spelling of the ING words below.

These families spell by the Verb Family Plan on page 54, for Root Verbs that end with 2 consonants.

thank	belong	scoff	bump	bang	cluck	blink
thanks	belongs	scoffs	bumps	bangs	clucks	blinks
_____	_____	_____	_____	_____	_____	_____
thanked	belonged	scoffed	bumped	banged	clucked	blinked

These families spell by the Verb Family Plan on page 56, for Root Verbs that end with 1 consonant.

snap	drop	nod	rub	step	stun	rip
snaps	drops	nods	rubs	steps	stuns	rips
_____	_____	_____	_____	_____	_____	_____
snapped	dropped	nodded	rubbed	stepped	stunned	ripped

These families spell by the Verb Family Plan on page 58, for Root Verbs that end with the letter E.

buckle	merge	scribble	plunge	rinse	crumble	emerge
buckles	merges	scribbles	plunges	rinses	crumbles	emerges
_____	_____	_____	_____	_____	_____	_____
buckled	merged	scribbled	plunged	rinsed	crumbled	emerged

Can you spell the ING Verbs for these Root Verbs?

risk	nap	scramble	slam	tickle	blend
_____	_____	_____	_____	_____	_____

The first 3 Verb Families in each section below, spell by one of the 3 plans you have been practicing.

All the other Verb Families in each section below have one word that does not spell by the plan.

For each family, use a pencil to lightly circle the word in that family that does not spell by the plan.

These families spell by the Verb Family Plan on page 54, for Root Verbs that end with 2 consonants.

block	last	rent	sing	sink	drink	sting	stink
blocks	lasts	rents	sings	sinks	drinks	stings	stinks
blocking	lasting	renting	singing	sinking	drinking	stinging	stinking
blocked	lasted	rented	sang	sank	drank	stung	stunk

These families spell by the Verb Family Plan on page 56, for Root Verbs that end with 1 consonant.

snip	kid	fan	run	sit	put	get	let
snips	kids	fans	runs	sits	puts	gets	lets
snipping	kidding	fanning	running	sitting	putting	getting	letting
snipped	kidded	fanned	ran	sat	put	got	let

These families spell by the Verb Family Plan on page 58, for Root Verbs that end with the letter E.

nurse	cackle	cringe	give
nurses	cackles	cringes	gives
nursing	cackling	cringing	giving
nursed	cackled	cringed	gave

In the Verb Families that had a word that did not spell by the plan, which word was not "by the plan?"

In every Verb Family with a word not spelled "by the plan," it is the Past Verb that is not "by the plan."

Can you make your own page, with all the same directions, but with new Verb Families as examples?

Where can you look to choose new Verb Families that will be good examples for each section?

To the right of each sentence, write the Root Verb of the first Past Verb you see in that sentence.

I saw an old cartoon that had lots of animals in it.   _____

A bee stung a dog and the dog began to bark and run.   _____

When the dog ran away barking, it scared an old cat that lay there in the sun.   _____

The bell rang on the cat's collar as the scared cat ran faster than the barking dog. _____

A sleeping bird woke up and sang a song that woke up every other animal.   _____

The animals sang and barked, ran and hopped, rang bells and jumped fences.   _____

They were all scared from being woken up suddenly by other scared animals.   _____

Then they each got more scared from seeing all the others be scared.   _____

The birds bumped into each other and fell from the sky.   _____

The ducks bumped into each other and sank in their pond.   _____

Some dogs sang crying songs back and forth and others barked in the darkness. _____

Each blank below is attached to a Root Verb. Write its Past Verb in the blank.

Then compare it with the story above.

I see_____ an old cartoon that had lots of animals in it.

A bee sting_____ a dog and the dog began to bark and run.

When the dog run_____ away barking, it scared an old cat that lay there in the sun.

The bell ring_____ on the cat's collar as the scared cat ran faster than the barking dog.

A sleeping bird wake_____ up and sang a song that woke up every other animal.

The animals sing_____ and bark_____, run_____ and hop_____,

                                                ring_____ bells and jump _____ fences.

They were all scare_____ from being woken up suddenly by other scared animals.

Then they each got more scare_____ from seeing all the others be scared.

The birds bump_____ into each other and fell from the sky.

The ducks bump_____ into each other and sank in their pond.

Some dogs sing_____ crying songs back and forth, others bark_____ in the darkness.

How can you check the Root Verbs you wrote in the right-side blanks at the top of this page?

We call this   **Learner's Choice Spelling Quiz** .   (L = Learner,   R = Reader)

Use this activity to practice spelling, using Verb Family Lists from any page in this book.

L and R each have a blank sheet of paper. Fold L's paper twice each direction for 16 (4x4) squares.

L picks a Verb Family from any page L chooses and L reads all 4 words in the Verb Family to R.

R covers page with R's paper and says the 4 words, pausing as L spells each word on L's paper.

After each word, R moves R's paper so that L can see that word, but not the next word in family.

L looks at R's paper to check spelling of each word before R says next word.

L puts all 4 words of a Verb Family in one folded square of L's paper, a different family in each square.

Complete 8 Verb Families on top half of L's paper, then fold the top half under the bottom half.

Spell the same 8 Verb Families. Check each family as you finish spelling it, instead of each word.

That is   **Learner's Choice Spelling Quiz.**

We call this   **Verb Ears Challenge.**   (L = Learner,   R = Reader)

L picks a Verb Family from any page L chooses and L reads all 4 words in the Verb Family to R.

R says a sentence using any one of the Verbs in the same Verb Family L just chose and read.

L listens to sentence as R says it. L says the Verb R used in the sentence, its Root Verb, and its ending.

Do this for 2 Verbs in each chosen Verb Family. L chooses to spell the Verb aloud or in L's Notebook.

That is   **Verb Ears Challenge.**

Celebrate finishing Chapter 2 by reading any or all of the following books.

The Red Tree   Shaun Tan
Where's Pup   Dayle Ann Dodds, Pierre Pratt
I am a little giraffe.   Francois Crozat
I Read Signs   Tara Hoban
Milet Picture Dictionary: English and others*   Sadat Turhan & others, Sally Hagin
    *(12 editions…1 English only, 11 bilingual editions: English and Albanian, Arabic,
Bengali, Chinese, French, German, Italian, Somali, Spanish, Turkish, Urdu & Vietnamese)

We recommend looking at what all the alphabets and languages look like. Enjoy comparing them.

If 1 of these is your native language & English a 2nd language, read the book often in both languages.

Chapter 3

Goals

Meet and practice (y) and the teams (gy ggy cy ce ci ey ay ie).
   (pp. 69 - 74 , 76 , 79 – 82 , 85 - 90)
See which word family lists are noun lists and which are verb lists.
   (pp. 73 , 75 , 79 - 80, 90)
Begin to recognize nouns and verbs in sentences.
   (pp. 74 - 81)
Study and practice when to use which member of a verb family.
   (pp. 74 – 78 , 80 - 81)
Practice spelling and using adjective families.
   (pp. 82 – 86 , 88 - 91)
Meet and practice using adjectives, articles and noun phrases.
   (pp. 82 – 89 , 91)

Here are some Practice Suggestions you may want to try.

This will be a good time for Learners to learn how to look words up in the dictionary.

The Reader can add a lot to the Learner's understanding of what is read by looking up some words.
Look up any words that have two or more commonly used meanings.
Look up any words about which you are in doubt about the pronunciation or meaning.
Read everything the dictionary says about a word: the syllables, the pronunciation, the families it's in.
For any verbs you look up, look at the spelling of all the forms of the verb, all 4 verbs in the verb family.
Do the same with adjective families and noun families .

The Reader should "think out loud" throughout the process of looking up a word and studying its entry.

Practice Calendar
Chapter 3

Day & Date	Time	Page	Notes, Comments

Why ask Y, "Why?" when Y already asks, "Why?"

Don't ask Y the "Why?" that Y is already asking!

I don't know "Why!"

I am Y.

Yell

I like to spell. Do you like to read?

Do you think it is easier to read, or easier to spell?

The easy way to make spelling easy for you is to read a lot, and then read some more.

Whenever you read, you are also watching someone spell well.

When you are reading, your brain is noticing how those well-spelled words are spelled.

As you read, your brain remembers how to spell some of the words, even if you are not trying to.

If you are trying to notice how to spell, your brain remembers more new spellings each time you read.

It is easier to read than to spell, but reading more will make spelling easier for you, and reading too.

I spell a lot of sounds.

I spell in many teams, CY, GY, AY, OY, EY, UY.

I team with A, E, O, and U. That is all the vowels except for I !   (I spell I's sounds by myself.)

I will teach you my CY and GY teams after I teach you the sounds I spell alone.

I am the only letter that can spell my own consonant sound and can also spell some vowel sounds!

R & L help vowels spell different vowel sounds in letter teams. for fur fir her all full

Vowels help consonants spell different consonant sounds in teams like CE, CI, CY, GE, GI & GY.

cent   city   mercy   gentle   urging   gyms

I spell in the vowel teams AY, OY, EY and UY, and the consonant teams CY and GY.

I am the only letter that can spell both, a consonant sound and also vowel sounds, by myself!

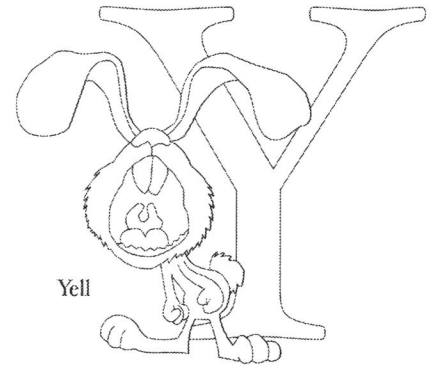

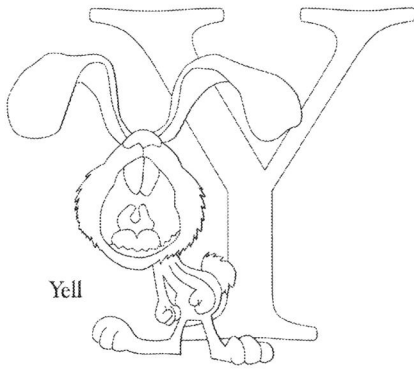

Yell

Y here again.

Teachers and scientists call me a consonant.

I do not have my own vowel sounds.

I do not spell a short sound that is my short sound.

I spell I's short sound or name sound in the middle of words.   rhythm   rhyme

I do not spell a name sound that is my name sound.

I spell E's name sound at the end of some words.   melody   funny

I spell I's name sound at the end of some words.   simplify   fly

All the real vowels have their own short sound and their own name sound.

I am a consonant, with my own consonant sound, the Y sound.   yes   yell

But other consonants can spell their consonant sounds **any** time, **any** place in a word!

I never spell my consonant sound to end a word, and rarely in the middle of a word.   mayor

I always spell my consonant sound when I begin a word.

In the middle of a root word, I almost always spell I's short sound or I's name sound.

When I end a root word with no vowels, I spell I's name sound, I work as a vowel, doing a vowel's job.

When I end a root word that has a prior vowel, I spell E's name sound, or I's name sound.

Listen as your Reader reads each Words List below. Which sound am I, Y, spelling in each Words List?

Can you read these lists after listening to your Reader read them? Or colorize the vowel sounds?

you	yap	gypsy	beyond	very	valley	apply	try	my
yet	yip	mystery	mayor	city	volley	supply	cry	by
Yeti	yum	byte	crayon	silly	pulley	petrify	fry	why

You can practice reading me, Y, in these Words Lists.

yes	yip	merry	Sally	sunny	money	funky	mystery
yams	yen	berry	silly	funny	monkey	handy	gypsy
yell	yin	very	Willy	runny	donkey	simply	cyst
yet	yan	many	hilly	tummy	turkey	smugly	gym
yammer	yap	marry	Larry	mommy	key	rusty	rhythmic

Now I will tell you about how I team with G.

When I team with G, G spells the J sound instead of the G sound G usually spells.

And I spell the same middle-of-the-word and end-of-the-word vowel sounds I usually spell.

Here are some examples.

Read them, then underline my GY team in each word.

gym	energy	stodgy	gyp	grungy	gym
gyp	clergy	edgy	gyps	grungier	gyms
gypsy	grungy		gypping	grungiest	
			gypped		gymnastics

But I do not always team with G when I follow G.

If there are two Gs side by side, I do not team with them! The two Gs spell the G sound.

Here are some examples where I follow two Gs, but do not team with G.

soggy   baggy   buggy   foggy   muggy   Ziggy

The GG team always spells a G sound, and tells you the 1 prior vowel spells a short vowel sound.

A soggy dog with a wagging tail jumped out from behind a parked car at a startled jogger.

Y again.

When I follow C, I always team with C.

C spells the S sound when I team with C.

C wanted to keep it easy for you at first, and did not tell you.

Yell

But now you are getting to be a pretty good reader.

You are learning to practice making choices between different sounds a letter might spell.

You are beginning to learn to recognize some of our Letter teams, and to read them.

So you are ready to read C's teams with me and I and E.

Do you remember that when the GE team is at the end of a word, the E at the end spells silence?

| urge | bulge | judge | edge | bridge | badge | fudge | singe | merge |

It works the same way with the CE team.   dance   fence   since

If you see the CE team at the end of a word, then the E spells silence.

Here are some words to help you practice reading the CY, CE and CI teams.

After you read each Words List, underline the team you practiced in that list.

fence	fancy	Nancy	pencil	accent	accident	access	entrance
convince	cyst	Tracy	city	cent	incident	excess	surface
dance	mercy	Lucy	dancing	recent	convincing	except	sentence

You have just begun to learn a lot of clues and rules for different sounds we letters spell.

It seems hard when you just hear about them. It gets easier as you practice reading or spelling them.

Every time you read, you practice seeing and using letter teams.

The way to make spelling easy is to read a lot, and then read some more.

Before starting this page, re-read all the Words Lists on pages 70 to 72.

Some of those words were root verbs. Some of those words were root nouns.

Here are the verb families of some root verbs you read on pages 70 to 72.

yip	yap	yell	dance	prance	fence	mince	gyp
yips	yaps	yells	dances	prances	fences	minces	gyps
yipping	yapping	yelling	dancing	prancing	fencing	mincing	gypping
yipped	yapped	yelled	danced	pranced	fenced	minced	gypped

urge	bulge	judge	edge	bridge	verge	merge	rhyme
urges	bulges	judges	edges	bridges	verges	merges	rhymes
urging	bulging	judging	edging	bridging	verging	merging	rhyming
urged	bulged	judged	edged	bridged	verged	merged	rhymed

Here are the noun families of some root nouns you read on pages 70 to 72.

yam	yell	rhyme	byte	mystic	key	monkey	money	fly
yams	yells	rhymes	bytes	mystics	keys	monkeys	monies	flies

yip	yap	rhythm	mystery	valley	volley	pulley	city	cry	try
yips	yaps	rhythms	mysteries	valleys	volleys	pulleys	cities	cries	tries

dance	fence	berry	trance	pencil	recess	accident	judge	bridge
dances	fences	berries	trances	pencils	recesses	accidents	judges	bridges

Can you colorize the vowel sounds on this page?

Use page 187 to choose tools and symbols.

Use page 192 to check your colorizing when you are done.

When you read page 73, were any of the words in the noun families also in the verb families?

Some words can only be used as Nouns. Some words can only be used as Verbs.

A lot of words can be used as a Noun or a Verb.

When you use the word to mean an action, you are using it as a Verb.

When you use the word to mean a creature, a place, or a thing, you are using the word as a Noun.

A word is not a Noun or a Verb until you use it as a Noun, or you use it as a Verb.

Which is the word, "dance," a place you go to, or the action you do there?

If you say "dance" meaning the place, it is a Noun.

If you say "dance" meaning the action, it is a Verb.

Which is the word, "fly," the buzzing bug, a creature, or the way the buzzing bug travels, an action?

When a Root Verb is a Root Noun, the Noun is often a creature or thing who does the action.

In the sentences below, which are in *italics*, nouns or verbs? Which are **bold**, nouns or verbs?

We began to *dance* the minute we got to the **dance.**

I am getting buggy from the buzzing of that **fly** as it *flies* in circles above my dinner.

My dog *yips* and *yaps* at my cat until her **yips** and **yaps** bug my dad, who yells at the dog.

When my dad *yells* at my yapping dog, dad's **yells** stop my dog from yipping and yapping.

A **bridge** *bridges* the water that it goes over.

Bridges *bridge* the distance from one spot to another spot, going over the spots between.

We put up a **fence** to *fence* in our dog, so he will not run off, or bother others.

We had to pick a **judge** to *judge* our fudge contest, but the **judge** cannot be in the contest.

An **edger** is a thing that *edges* the **edge** of the grass or the **edge** of a hedge.

"Pill" and "fill" *rhyme*, and "big" and "pig" *rhyme,* but a **rhyme** has sentences that *rhyme.*

"Five, six, pick up sticks," is a **rhyme.** What two words in that sentence *rhyme?*

Whenever I mince onions, I start to *cry*, and my sister tells me to, "have a good **cry.**"

The tube in my bike tire was beginning to *bulge.* The **bulge** in the tire kept getting bigger.

In the above sentences, a **bold** word is a **Noun** and a word in *italics* is a *Verb.*

Here are some other verb families and noun families that have the same, or related, root words.

gift	give	cover	cover	glove	glove	jog	jog
gifts	gives	covers	covers	gloves	gloves	jogs	jogs
giver	giving		covering	gloving		jogger	jogging
givers	gave		covered	gloved		joggers	jogged

flop	flop	flip	flip	vent	vent	jump	jump
flops	flops	flips	flips	vents	vents	jumps	jumps
	flopping	flipper	flipping		venting		jumping
	flopped	flippers	flipped		vented		jumped

struggle	struggle	pledge	pledge	lodge	lodge	stick	stick
struggles	struggles	pledges	pledges	lodges	lodges	sticks	sticks
	struggling		pledging	lodger	lodging	sticker	sticking
	struggled		pledged	lodgers	lodged	stickers	stuck

juggler	juggle	tangle	tangle	jingle	jingle	giggle	giggle
jugglers	juggles	tangles	tangles	jingles	jingles	giggles	giggles
	juggling		tangling		jingling	giggler	giggling
	juggled		tangled		jingled	gigglers	giggled

Take turns with your Reader making sentences with the words in these noun and verb Families.

First say the word, then say a sentence using the word.

When your Reader says the word and sentence, you say if the word is a noun or verb in that sentence.

When you say the word and sentence, your Reader can say if you used the word as a noun or a verb.

At first it will be hard for you. The more you listen to and think about sentences, the easier it will get.

What does the word **mean** in that sentence? Is it an action, or is it a place or thing or creature?

We won't tell you all about nouns & verbs now, but you can begin to practice hearing and using them.

It's like anything else you learn; the more you practice it, the easier it gets.

These Verb Family Stories will help you practice seeing the verbs and nouns in the sentences you read.

In <u>each</u> story below, which are in *italics*, nouns or verbs? Which are **bold**, nouns or verbs?

My dad asked me to *fence* our property with a tall **fence**.

Fencing the property with a **fence** will stop other animals from bothering our cats or dogs.

First I suggested we *fence* the property with a thick hedge, but animals get under hedges.

I *fenced* our property with a tall, strong **fence**, instead of hedges.

My dog likes to *yelp*. She *yelps* too often, my dad says. Dad does not like her **yelps**.

I *yelp* with my dog, but only if my dad is not home. My dog and I both like *yelping*.

Last month, we *yelped* every week. Last week, we *yelped* every day that dad was gone.

My dog *yips* and *yaps* as often as she *yelps*. Dad says her **yips**, **yaps** and **yelps** bug him.

My dog just likes *yipping* and *yapping* and *yelping*. But my dad does not like *yelling*.

There is a **fiddler** in my village. She *fiddles* at the mall every day.

The **fiddler** *fiddles* on her **fiddle**, and her pal *fiddles* with her.

Citizens passing by stop to listen to the two **fiddlers** *fiddling* on their **fiddles**.

Some citizens thank the **fiddlers** by putting a dollar or two in the **fiddler's** hat.

I saw two listeners put a five dollar bill in the **fiddler's** hat as the **fiddlers** *fiddled*.

I thanked the **fiddlers** as I put a dollar in the **fiddler's** hat, and the **fiddlers** thanked me.

I can't *fiddle* at all, but I like the **fiddling** of the two **fiddlers**, so I thank them for it.

Some day I want to *fiddle* like they can *fiddle*. I think *fiddling* must be a lot of fun.

My mom likes to **dance**. She **dances** whenever she can. She even **dances** with no music!

I **dance** with her often. I like **dancing** also. We both like **dancing**, so we **dance** together.

But my mom goes to *dances*. At a *dance* there is a band making music to **dance** to.

When I get bigger, mom will take me to a *dance* so I can **dance** to music from a band.

Last month I **danced** every week, and last week I **danced** every day, but never at a *dance*.

In every story above except one, **Nouns** were **bold** and *Verbs* were in *italics*.

Which is the one story on the page in which **Verbs** were **bold** and *Nouns* were in *italics*?

Can you put the correct verb from each verb family into each blank in the stories below?

You may want to re-read a story on page 76 before you fill in its missing words below.

fence	dance	fiddle
fences	dances	fiddles
fencing	dancing	fiddling
fenced	danced	fiddled

My dad asked me to _____ our property with a tall **fence**.

_____ the property with a **fence** will stop animals from bothering our cats or dogs.

I said to _____ the property with a thick hedge, but animals can get under hedges.

I _____ our property with a tall, strong **fence**, instead of hedges.

My mom likes to _____. She _____ often. She even _____ with no music!

I _____ with her. I like _____. We both like _____, so we _____ together.

But my mom goes to **dances**. At a **dance** there is a band making music to _____ to.

When I get bigger, mom will take me to a **dance** so I can _____ to music from a band.

Last month I _____ every week, and last week I _____ often, but not at a **dance**.

There is a **fiddler** in my village. She _____ at the mall every day.

The **fiddler** _____ on her **fiddle**, and her pal _____ with her.

Citizens passing by stop to listen to the two **fiddlers** _____ on their **fiddles**.

Some citizens thank the **fiddlers** by putting a dollar or two in the **fiddler's** hat.

I saw two listeners put a five dollar bill in the **fiddler's** hat as the **fiddlers** _____.

I thanked the **fiddlers** as I put a dollar in the **fiddler's** hat, and the **fiddlers** thanked me.

I can't _____ at all, but I like the **fiddling** of the two **fiddlers**, so I thank them for it.

I want to _____ like they can _____. I think _____ must be a lot of fun.

After you have filled in the blanks, re-read page 76, then re-read this page to check your choices.

With each story below, decide whether the <u>underlined</u> words are all nouns in that story, or all verbs.

My mother cooks <u>yams</u> for supper. I ate one <u>yam</u>. My brother ate three <u>yams</u>.

All together, my brother and I ate four <u>yams</u>. One <u>yam</u> plus three <u>yams</u> is four <u>yams</u>.

I <u>lodge</u> in a cottage in my village. My parents <u>lodge</u> in a cottage next door.

My brother <u>lodges</u> in the cottage one cottage beyond my parent's cottage.

My sisters <u>lodge</u> in another lodge. They make a living renting lodges to lodgers.

The lodges the lodgers <u>lodge</u> in are small, but inexpensive. Inexpensive things cost less.

Many lodgers like <u>lodging</u> in a place that is inexpensive to <u>lodge</u> in.

My job is to be a judge. I <u>judge</u> crimes. I have <u>judged</u> crimes for many years.

Since I am called a judge, I get a lot of calls asking me to <u>judge</u> contests.

I get asked to <u>judge</u> pig contests, dog contests, dance contests, and even coloring contests.

Last year I got asked to <u>judge</u> a surfing contest. Since I do not surf, I do not <u>judge</u> surfing.

I think I am better at <u>judging</u> jellies and jams than I am at <u>judging</u> pigs and dogs.

I like to dance, and I like to <u>judge</u> jazz dancing, but I have not <u>judged</u> any other dances.

But I am best at <u>judging</u> crimes, not contests. <u>Judging</u> crimes is my job. I'm a judge.

I like to <u>yell</u> a lot, but when I <u>yell</u> a lot my mother asks me not to <u>yell</u>. So I don't <u>yell</u>.

But some days I forget not to <u>yell</u> after she asks me to stop <u>yelling</u>, so then she <u>yells</u> at me.

When my mother <u>yells</u> at me for <u>yelling</u> a lot, what she <u>yells</u> is, "Stop <u>yelling</u> or else!"

Yesterday, when she <u>yelled</u> at me to stop <u>yelling</u>, I <u>yelled</u> back at her, "Stop <u>yelling</u> at me!"

Then she was mad. Did she stop <u>yelling</u> at me? What do you think? Do you ever <u>yell</u>?

Re-read the page.

After each story, say what clues told you that the underlined words were nouns or verbs.

Pick a story that you wish to continue. Copy it first, or not, then add to it in your notebook.

Can you tell a story that uses all 4 verbs from one family from any of the prior pages?

Are these 2-word families verb families or noun families?

yam	yell	yap	yip	yelp	dance	accent	accident	fence
yams	yells	yaps	yips	yelps	dances	accents	accidents	fences

pencil	cent	scent	gym		key	turkey	alley	valley
pencils	cents	scents	gyms		keys	turkeys	alleys	valleys

Here is a story using two of the noun families in the bottom set of noun families above.

Read the story, then <u>underline</u> the nouns from the two noun families that are used in the story below.

My cat likes to visit with other cats in the alley by the gym.

I live by the gym, and it does not cost any money to go to the gym that I live by.

The city I live in pays to have all the gyms open for all of the kids and adults to play in.

It does not cost my cat any money to visit with other cats in the alley by the gym.

There are a lot of alleys in my city, but not as many gyms as alleys.

In noun families, S at the end of the word means "more than one."

When a noun ends with Y after a consonant, you do more than add S to mean "more than one."

city	mystery	berry	tummy	gypsy	ferry		key	alley	valley
cities	mysteries	berries	tummies	gypsies	ferries		keys	alleys	valleys

If E's name sound is spelled by Y to end a root noun, replace Y with IE when you add S.

In "key," "alley" and "valley," E's name sound is spelled by the EY team, so you only add S.

If Y spells I's name sound to end a noun, Y still needs to be replaced with IE when you add S.

fly	sky	fry	sty	cry	try	supply
flies	skies	fries	sties	cries	tries	supplies

Here are examples of the Verb Family Spelling Plan for verb families whose root verb ends with Y.

hurry	worry	ferry	bury	carry	marry	vary
hurries	worries	ferries	buries	carries	marries	varies
hurrying	worrying	ferrying	burying	carrying	marrying	varying
hurried	worried	ferried	buried	carried	married	varied

Whether root verbs end with a Y spelling I's name sound or E's, their families spell by the same plan.

In the IES and IED endings, an IE team spells whichever name sound Y spelled in the root verb.

fly	fry	try	cry	pry	dry	supply
flies	fries	tries	cries	pries	dries	supplies
flying	frying	trying	crying	prying	drying	supplying
flew	fried	tried	cried	pried	dried	supplied

On page 79, you saw some noun families end with an EY team spelling E's name sound.

Some of those noun families have verb families with the same root word. Some don't.

key	key	volley	volley	turkey	alley	valley
keys	keys	volleys	volleys	turkeys	alleys	valleys
	keying		volleying		donkey	monkey
	keyed		volleyed		donkeys	monkeys

Volley ball players have to "volley for serve," hit the volley ball back and forth until one team misses. The team that did not miss gets to serve first.

If you ask the score as they volley for serve, they will say they are only "volleying for serve." (verb)

If you ask immediately after they volley for serve, they will say they just now "volleyed for serve." (verb)

When someone says, "That was a good volley," hitting the ball back and forth is a volley.   (noun)

If you do it again, that is "two good volleys." Nouns can be made plural.   (noun)

These stories can help you practice recognizing nouns and verbs.

A locksmith *keys* **locks**. The locksmith puts the new **lock** in the door.

Usually the **keys** that fit the new **lock** come in the same package the new lock comes in.

Sometimes, maybe if the **keys** get lost, the locksmith has to make the new **keys**.

Making new **keys** for an old or new **lock** is called *keying* the **lock**, or *rekeying* the **lock**.

When the **lock** is in the door, the locksmith gives you the **keys**. The **lock** has been *keyed*.

You do not *key* the door when you use the **key** in the **lock**.

You can use your **key** to *lock* the door, or to *unlock* the door.

But you cannot *key* the door, the locksmith does that. You only *lock* the door, or *unlock* it.

But the word "key" is used for other meanings also.

A paper with the answers to a test is called "the answer **key**."

A long, thin bit of sand sticking up out of a big body of water is called a "**key**."

A grand piano has 88 **keys.** You press the piano's **keys** to play music on the piano.

Those are some of the different ways we use the word "key." There are many others.

Do you have a **supply** of pencils and paper? Did your parents *supply* you with them?

I keep myself *supplied* with pens and pencils and paper. When I use them up, I get more.

Many schools *supply* kids with pencils and paper, many schools do not.

If the school does not *supply* school **supplies**, families go to a store to *supply* the **supplies**.

Having an extra **supply** of school **supplies** lets you go to the store less often to *re-supply*.

Who *supplies* your family with food and drinks and medicine? Where do you *re-supply*?

Have you ever been on a picnic? What **supplies** do you *supply* yourself with for a picnic?

In our stories in this book, we have used a few words with sounds or teams you have not met yet.

Are you getting better at figuring out new words by using the sense of the rest of the sentence?

Can you work as a team to tell Verb Family Stories or Noun Family Stories for other root words?

Y

Yell

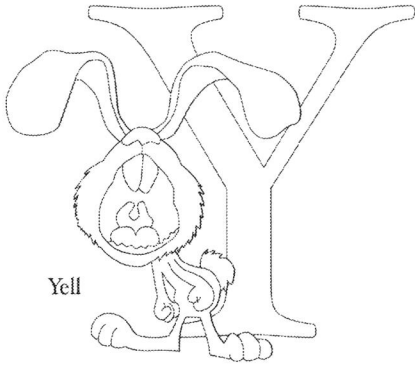

Many words that end with me, Y, are Adjectives.

The job an Adjective does is to tell you more about a Noun.

Adjectives describe qualities of Nouns.

Usually, not always, if a Noun has an Adjective,

the Adjective is the word before that Noun in the sentence.

Do you remember what a Noun is?   A Noun is the word for a place, a thing or a creature.

Here are some 3-word Noun Phrases.

The whole Phrase tells about the Noun in a 3-word Noun Phrase, but only one word **is** the Noun.

The *Adjective* in each of the 3-word Noun Phrases below is in *italics*.

a *big* dog   my *red* socks   seven *flying* birds   its *flapping* wings

a *sunny* day   that *hungry* cat   some *hot* peppers

Noun Phrases can have more than one Adjective. We can list the **Adjectives**.

that **big red** dog   several **hungry, squirmy, black** squid   a **warm sunny** sky

lots of **big, smelly, hissing, angry** skunks   a **bigger, smellier, angrier** skunk

a **low slow** pitch   the **biggest, smelliest, angriest** skunk   a **small yellow** bird

You have practiced how the 2 words in a noun family mean "one" or "more than one" of the noun.

You have practiced & thought about which of the 4 verbs in a verb family to use when you use verbs.

Which verb in a verb family you choose depends on **who** is *doing* the *verb's* action, & **when** they do it.

Adjective Families with 3 words tell how strong that quality is in that noun.

In these 3-word Adjective Families, which word says the quality is **most** strong, the 1st, 2nd or 3rd?

funny	happy	sunny	foggy	silly	sloppy	soggy
funnier	happier	sunnier	foggier	sillier	sloppier	soggier
funniest	happiest	sunniest	foggiest	silliest	sloppiest	soggiest

The ER word in an Adjective Family means "even more so" than the Root Adjective's meaning.

The EST word in an Adjective Family means this noun is "the most" of the Root Adjective's meaning.

You can practice reading and spelling the Adjectives on this page. Can you use them in sentences?

big	red	thin	sad	hot	small	long
bigger	redder	thinner	sadder	hotter	smaller	longer
biggest	reddest	thinnest	saddest	hottest	smallest	longest

Did you notice that in the 5 Adjective Families to the left, we repeat the last letter to add "er" and "est."
You will learn **why** we do that in Chapter 5, but we will tell you **when** to do that now.

Repeat the last letter of the Root Adjective before adding "er" or "est" if, and only if:

the last letter is a single consonant following 1 prior vowel spelling a "short" vowel sound.

The Adjective Families below are one-word Adjective Families.

With a one-word Adjective Family the words "more" and "most" do the job of ER and EST endings.

a *rotten* apple	some *placid* cats	that *rigid* spring
a more *rotten* apple	a more *placid* cat	a more *rigid* spring
the most *rotten* apple	the most *placid* cat	the most *rigid* spring

a *boring* story   an *interesting* story

a more *boring* story   a more *interesting* story

the most *boring* story   the most *interesting* story

a *helpful* hint   a *tactful* reply

a more *helpful* helper than I am   a more *tactful* reply than mine

the most *helpful* helper of all   her most *tactful* reply yet

Does the word "more" do the same job as the ER ending, or the EST ending?

Take turns making sets like those above **or** 3 Noun Phrases that use 1 Adjective Family's 3 Adjectives.

We call these **Adjective Family Stories**.

In each story, fill the blanks using words from one Adjective Family.

Use the sense of the sentence and story to decide which Adjective to put in each blank.

Jeff is *biggest*. None of us are *bigger*. None of us are as *big*.

Jim is *big* also, but he is the *smallest* of the four of us.

None of us are *smaller* than Jim, but Jazmin is as *small*, so she is also the *smallest* of us.

Jim is _____. Janet is _____ than Jim. Jeff is the _____ of us.

My frog is _____, for a frog. My cat is _____. My dog is my _____ pet.

My dad says I am getting _____. I am _____ than I was when I was six.

My dad is not *thin*, but he is trying to get *thin*.

Since the day he began trying to get *thinner*, he is beginning to get *thinner*.

My dad is trying to get as _____ as my mom. Mom is the *thinnest* adult in our family.

I am the *thinnest* person in our family, but dad is not trying to get as _____ as me.

Each missing 2-word phrase below is "more" or "most" followed by an Adjective from a 1-word family.

My brother said yesterday was the *most boring* day of our summer.

Then my sister said last Thursday was even *more boring* than yesterday.

So they began to argue about which day was our *most boring* day of summer.

I think their argument about the _____ _____ day of our summer is *boring*.

I think it is the _____ _____ thing we have done all summer long.

If they argue all day about _____ days, today will be our _____ _____ day.

I like to help. It is fun being *helpful*. My parents say I am a *helpful* son and brother.

I like to try to learn how to do more things. When I learn more things, I get *more helpful*.

I get *more helpful* every month than I was the month before, as I learn more ways to help.

I like to be the _____ _____ person I can, but sometimes I am not.

There is a lot to tell about adjectives.

I, Y, end many Root Adjectives.

When Y ends a family's root word the family spells "by the Y plan."

"By the Y plan," for adjectives, means Y changes to I when ER or EST ends an Adjective.

Practice reading and spelling these Adjective Families. Can you use them in sentences?

happy	grumpy	silly	funny	merry	angry	messy
happier	grumpier	sillier	funnier	merrier	angrier	messier
happiest	grumpiest	silliest	funniest	merriest	angriest	messiest

empty	sunny	foggy	yummy	fancy	dingy	dusty
emptier	sunnier	foggier	yummier	fancier	dingier	dustier
emptiest	sunniest	foggiest	yummiest	fanciest	dingiest	dustiest

Write a check (✓) by endings that say "more than others." Underline endings that say "the most." Check your work above on page 184.

An Adjective and a Noun have to "agree." What does that mean? Are they going to talk or argue? No. A Noun and its Adjective "agree" when that Adjective makes sense with that Noun.

Which make sense? Which do not?

that singing pencil	her dirty hands	his black cat	a happy log
that singing bird	her foggy hands	his purple cat	a happy dog

that silly wall	a foggy day	a funny comment
that sturdy wall	a foggy log	a funny coffin

a sunny sky	a spelling frog	an angry pencil	an empty glass
a sunny fog	a spelling book	an angry bull	an empty pencil

The phrases below are examples of 3-word Noun Phrases whose one Adjective and one Noun agree.

that singing bird   her dirty hands   his black cat   a happy dog

that sturdy wall   a foggy day   a funny comment

a sunny sky   a spelling book   an angry bull   an empty glass

The Noun Phrases above, whose Nouns and Adjectives "agree," are all from the bottom of page 85.

Each was paired on page 85 with a Noun Phrase whose Adjective did not make sense with its Noun.

Can you say why those Adjectives and Nouns that did not "agree" did not make sense together?

Where Adjective and Noun disagree, can you change the Adjectives so they agree?

What about the Noun?

These Adjective Stories each use all 3 kinds of words that can be used in an Adjective Family.

Read these Adjective Stories, then make up your own.

We wanted to go swimming on a sunny day.   I gave a silly response.

We wanted to go on a sunnier day than today.   Sal gave a sillier response.

Today was not the sunniest day to go swimming.   Then I gave the silliest response yet.

He runs fast, but his sister runs faster. Their brother is the fastest runner in their family.

His desk is empty and dusty.   I was ready two days ago.

Her desk is emptier and dustier.   I was even more ready yesterday.

The emptiest desk is the dustiest.   Now I am the most ready I have ever been.

In your Notebook, write a page of 3-word Noun Phrases that have one Adjective and one Noun.

Start each phrase with one of the words below. These words work as "Articles." Articles tell "which?"

a	her	this	no	a lot of	one	ten
an	his	these	any	lots of	two	twenty
the	my	that	few	many	three	thirty
each	your	those	several	most	four	forty-four
every	our	other	some	all	five	fifty-five

Can you, in your Notebook, write a page of Noun Phrases that have more than one Adjective?

Start each Noun Phrase with one of the Articles from page 86. Here are some examples.

this rigid sturdy wall   many happy funny movies   any big black dog

that big, furry, gray cat   these cute, purring, little kittens

our rustiest, dirtiest, fastest tractor   her big, empty, dusty desk   a dusty black rug

Did you remember, as you made your Noun Phrases, to choose Adjectives that "agree" with their Noun?

Did you notice that Articles need to "agree" with the Noun in the phrase also?

Some Articles mean "one" of the Noun, as part of that Article's meanings.   another cat

Some Articles mean "more than one" of the Noun, as part of that Article's meaning.   other cats

The Articles "that," "an," & "a" refer to **one** of a Noun, "some" & "many" refer to **more than one**.

In the pairs of Noun Phrases below, one phrase makes sense and the other does not make sense.

In Noun Phrases that do not make sense, the Article or the Adjective does not agree with the Noun.

For each pair of Noun Phrases, say which phrase does not make sense and why.

Is it the Article or the Adjective?

Which make sense?   Which do not?

Say why not!

a big black puppies   all pink and purple squirrels

a litter of puppies   that furry squirrel

those red pencils   her biggest book   any soft song

that red pencils   twenty funniest book   one silliest songs

these dusty red truck   a lot of fuzzy, furry kitten

this glittering purple truck   a hungry kitten

Take turns making sets (see end of pg. 83) of 3 Noun Phrases that use 3 Adjectives from any 1 family.

Skim or read pp. 84-87 to choose 3-word Adjective Families to use in your sets of Noun Phrases.

Can you <u>underline</u> all the Adjectives on this page?

Jimmy had a fancy pencil. Nancy had a fancier pencil. Jill had the fanciest pencil of all.

Ellie has a funny yell. Ziggy has a funnier yell. Felix has the funniest yell of them all.

Saturday was a foggy day. Sunday was a foggier day. Monday was the foggiest day yet.

Nancy and Jack danced a simple dance. Jill and Frank danced a simpler dance.

Justin and Janet danced a simpler dance than Jill and Frank or Nancy and Jack.

Vince and Valery danced the simplest dance of any of the dancers.

Some dancers were being silly when they danced.

The songs the band sang were sillier than the dancing of the dancers.

But the funny things the dancers yelled during the songs were the silliest silliness.

I love yams. Yams are yummy. Yams are yummier with melted butter mixed into them.

I love berries. Berries are yummier than yams, but berries are not yummier with butter.

But I love apple, orange, banana and blackberry salad best of all.

Apple, orange, banana and blackberry salad is the yummiest snack I love.

A small city can be dingy, dirty, smelly and grungy, even the smallest cities can.

Bigger cities can be dingier, dirtier, smellier and grungier than smaller cities.

The biggest cities can be the dingiest, dirtiest, smelliest and grungiest of all the cities.

On foggy days I am not very funny. On the days that are the sunniest, I am funniest.

If it is only a little foggy, and if it is not foggy very long, I get funnier.

Adjectives can tell a quality a noun has,   big dog

  compare that quality to other nouns,   biggest pet

  or compare that quality to the same quality in other nouns.   bigger cat than my cat

Adjectives help you picture a noun in your mind.

We blanked the ER and EST endings in these stories for you to fill in.

Read the whole story before you choose where to add ER or EST endings.

Underline the other word from the same Adjective Family, the Root Adjective that has no ending.

Then use this page to check your work on page 88, and use page 88 to check your work on this page.

Jim had a fancy pencil. Nancy had a fanc____ pencil. Jill had the fanc_____ pencil of all.

Ellie has a funny yell. Ziggy has a funn___ yell. Felix has the funn_____ yell of them all.

Saturday was a foggy day. Sunday was a fogg__ day. Monday was the fogg____ day yet.

Nancy and Jack danced a simple dance. Jill and Frank danced a simpler dance.

Justin and Janet danced a simpl___ dance than Jill and Frank or Nancy and Jack.

Vince and Valery danced the simpl____ dance of any of the dancers.

Some dancers were being silly when they danced.

The songs the band sang were sill___ than the dancing of the dancers.

But the funny things the dancers yelled during the songs were the sill_____ silliness.

I love yams. Yams are yummy. Yams are yummier with melted butter mixed into them.

I love berries. Berries are yum____ than yams, but berries are not yummier with butter.

But I love apple, orange, banana and blackberry salad best of all.

Apple, orange, banana and blackberry salad is the yumm_____ snack I love.

A small city can be dingy, dirty, smelly and grungy, even the small____ cities can.

Bigg___ cities can be ding____, dirt____, smell____ and grung____ than small___ cities.

The biggest cities can be the dingiest, dirtiest, smelliest and grungiest of all the cities.

On foggy days I am not very funny.

On the days that are the sunn_____, I am funn_____.

If it is only a little foggy, and if it is not foggy very long, I get funn____.

In Volume 1, and even more in Volume 2, you have figured out some words yourself.

You figured out words with letters you had not met yet, such as H and W.

> he   her   his   we   were   went

You figured out words with teams you had not met yet, such as TH, SH, WH and EE.

> the   this   that   she   what   when   see   bee   feel

When you figure out a word with a new team, do you learn what sound that team spells in that word?

You figured words out by listening to your Reader read the words as you looked at them.

You figured words out by using the sense of a sentence to read the sentence.

You remembered some words by practicing them again and again as soon as you learned them.

In Volume 2, most of our stories have a few words with letters or teams you have not met yet.

We did that so you can practice using the sense of a sentence to read new words.

Even Readers that know all the letters' & teams' sounds use the sense of a sentence for some words.

You have been reading the AY team since Volume 1.

> day   yesterday   Monday   Thursday   Saturday   Sunday   way   away   say

What vowel's name sound does the AY team spell?   _____

Here are some word families whose root words end with the AY team spelling A's name sound.

play	stay	pay	way	day	ray	gray	gay
plays	stays	pays	ways	days	rays	grayer	gayer
playing	staying	paying				grayest	gayest
played	stayed	paid					

Can you say which lists are Verb Families, which are Noun Families, & which are Adjective Families?

Can you work with your Reader as a team to make stories for some or all of those word families?

We call this   **Sentence Sense Re-runs.**

Go back to the pages that have stories on them. Re-read the stories.

As you read, find any words that were new to you when you read the story.

When you first saw some of those new words, you used the sense of the sentence to read them.

When you see a word that you used the sense of the sentence to read, write it in your Notebook.

Write the word's family. Colorize the vowels. Make up a sentence using the word.

Make up a different sentence for every word in that word's family. Take turns with your Reader.

That is called   **Sentence Sense Re-runs.**

We call this   **Noun Phrase Agreements.**   (L = Learner,   R = Reader)

Go back to the pages that have stories on them. Re-read the stories. Mark a check by each Adjective.

Down the left edge of a page in your Notebook list every Adjective in each story you read.

Take turns making up pairs of Noun Phrases that both use that same Adjective.

For 1 phrase use a Noun that makes sense with that Adjective, so that the Adjective and Noun "agree."

For the other phrase, use a Noun that does not make sense with that Adjective, so they "disagree."

Pick an Article that agrees with its Noun about "1" or "more than 1" to start each of your 2 phrases.

If L made up phrases, then R says which made sense and how the other phrase did not make sense.

If R made up phrases, then L says which made sense and how the other phrase did not make sense.

Is it easier to make funny phrases that do make sense, or funny phrases that do not make sense?

That is called   **Noun Phrase Agreements.**

Celebrate reading Chapter 3 by reading any or all of the following books.

Ruby's Wish   Shirin Yin Bridges, Sophie Blackall
Little Buggy   Kevin O'Malley
Amazing Grace   Mary Hoffman, Caroline Birch
A Fly Went By   Mike and Marshall McClintock
Little Rabbit's First Word Book Ever   Alan Baker

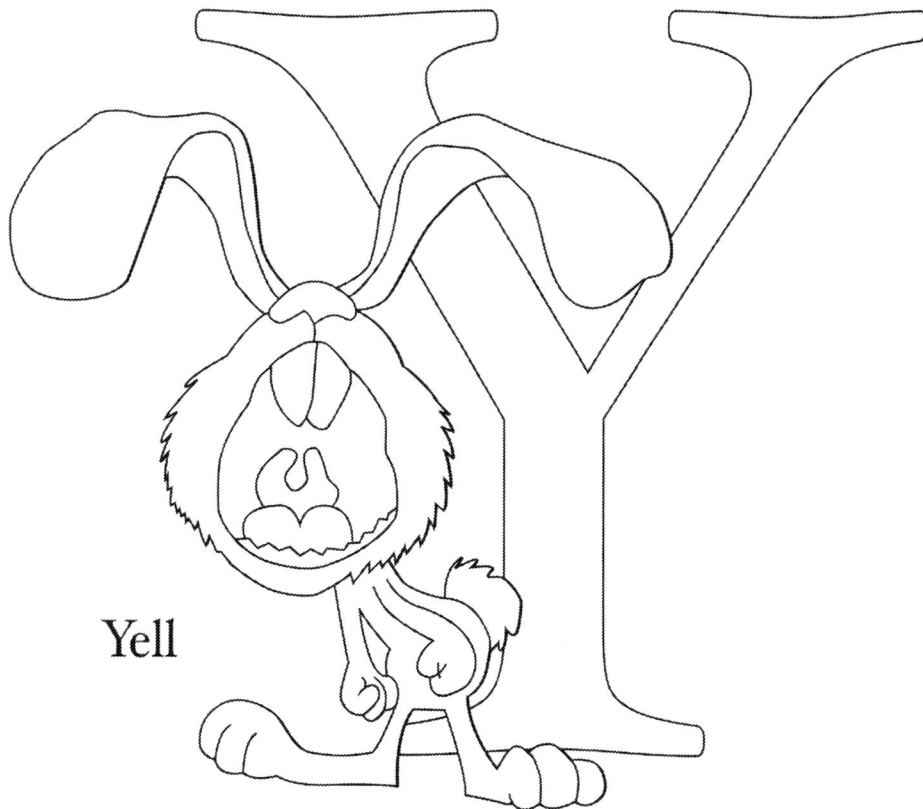

Yell

CHAPTER 4

Goals

Meet and practice (w q) and the team (qu).
(pp. 95 - 99 , 101 - 102)
Study and practice when to use which member of a verb family.
(pp. 96 - 97 , 100 - 109)
Focus on (-s) ending verbs and (-s) ending nouns.
(pp. 100 - 105)

<u>Here are some Practice Suggestions you may want to try</u>.

After reading a story the whole way through, go back and read the story a 2nd time, more slowly.

The 2nd time, pause after each sentence until L touches any action verb L sees in that sentence.

After touching the action verb, L says the root verb of the action verb's family.

This option is usable with any story in Volume 2 or 1, or any storybook.

Try this with other stories.

PRACTICE CALENDAR
CHAPTER 4

DAY & DATE	TIME	PAGE	NOTES, COMMENTS

My name is W. I am a consonant.

I team with other letters to spell several sounds.

I can team with vowels to help them spell vowel sounds.

So do R and L. We each team with vowels.

  or   far   fur   stir   fall   full   toll

Wall

You learned to read my W sound reading practice sentences with your Reader.

        we   was   went   will   were

Here are some easy words and sentences to practice.

wag	Wes	wall	well	wig
wags	wet	walls	welt	wit
wax	wed	Walt	weld	wilt
waxes	wets	Walt's	welds	will
waxing	weds	Walter	welts	willing

weld	wed
welds	weds
welding	wedding
welded	wedded

Will Wendy win? Wendy will win.

Will Walt win? Yes, Walter will win.

Will Will win? Will will win.

Wes and Will went west.

Will and Wes went to Wendy and Walt's wedding.

Will and Wes weld. Wes welds well. Will welds a little bit.

Walt wet Wes's walls, and Walt will wet Will's walls. Walt wets walls for a living.

When we went west we were wilting in the hot, windy western deserts.

Why did Walter's wax candles in the trunk of the car all melt when we crossed the desert?

The sentences on this page may help you think and talk about when to use each form of a verb.

The root verb of the verb family they illustrate is "swim." Its 4 forms are   swim
                                                                       swims
                                                                       swimming
                                                                       swam

I swim. You swim. We swim. They swim. He swims. She swims. The red dog swims.

I can swim. You can swim. We can swim. They can swim.

He can swim. She can swim. The red dog can swim.

I will swim after supper. She will swim after supper. Her dog will swim with us.

I swim after supper. She swims after supper. Her dog swims with us.

I swam after supper. She swam after supper. Her dog swam with us.

That dog swims. The dogs swim. That person swims. They all swim. Do cats swim?

I am swimming. I was swimming. I will be swimming. I love swimming and running.

You are swimming. You were swimming. You will be swimming. You love swimming.

He is swimming. He was swimming. He will be swimming. He loves swimming.

She is swimming. She was swimming. She will be swimming. She loves swimming.

We are swimming. We were swimming. We will be swimming. We love swimming.

They are swimming. They were swimming. They will be swimming.

I swam yesterday. You swam yesterday. He swam yesterday. She swam yesterday.

That big dog swam yesterday and today. That big dog swims every day.

My sister swam yesterday and today. My sister swims every Saturday and Sunday.

My brother will be swimming next Monday and Thursday. He swims two days per week.

My mother will swim every Sunday and Monday this month.

Last month, she swam every Saturday and Sunday with my sister.

Use a different verb family to replace the "swim" family as you re-read the page.

Do the sentences still make sense when you use the new verb family instead of the "swim" family?

Without looking at page 96, use the sense of the sentences to fill in the missing words below.

When you are done, use the sentences on page 96 to check your answers.

I swim. You swim. We swim. They swim. He swims. She _____ . The red dog swims.

I can swim. You can swim. We can swim. They can swim.

He can _____ . She _____ swim. The red dog can swim.

I will swim after supper. She will swim after supper. Her dog will _____ with us.

I swim after supper. She swims after supper. Her dog _____ with us.

I swam after supper. She swam after supper. Her dog _____ with us.

The dog swims. The dogs swim. That person _____ . They _____ . Do cats?

I am swimming. I was swimming. I will be _____. I love swimming.

You are swimming. You were swimming. You _____ be swimming.

He is swimming. He was swimming. He will be swimming. He loves _____.

She is swimming. She was swimming. She will ____ swimming. She loves swimming.

We are swimming. We were swimming. We will be swimming. We love _____.

They are swimming. They were swimming. They will be swimming.

I swam yesterday. You swam yesterday. He swam yesterday. She _____ yesterday.

That big dog _____ yesterday and today. That big dog swims every day.

My sister swam yesterday and today. My sister _____ every Saturday and Sunday.

My brother will be _____ next Monday and Thursday. He swims 2 days a week.

My mother will _____ every Sunday and Monday this month.

Last month, she _____ every Saturday and Sunday with my sister.

I'm Q. Quite pleased to meet you.

I always work with my only teammate U.

We always spell our same sound.

Really, K and W could do all our work.

It's their sounds that U and I spell!

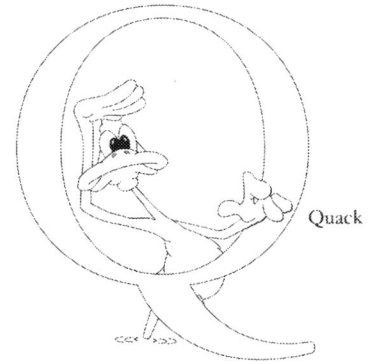

"letters   Q + U   =   K + W   sounds"   That's the math I use for my job.

You know how shy K is about spelling K's sound. Some even say K is lazy!

I guess they say that because K has help from C spelling K's sound.   tickets   blocks

But I am glad K and W let me, Q, and my partner, U, spell K and W's sounds sometimes.

I am thankful to K and W! And thankful to U for being in a team with me.

Here are some words and sentences you can use to practice reading Q + U (= K + W).

| quit | squid | quill | squint | quilt | squirt |
| quick | quickly | quack | squiggle | quiz | squirrel |

In my class we had a quick quiz.

The squirmy squid quickly squirted a lot of black liquid. Then the squid hid under it.

Squids squirt an inky liquid whenever they get attacked. They squirt it when they are scared.

When a squid squirts its inky, black liquid, is it having fun playing in the summer sun?

What is it a squid wants when the squid squirts its black, inky liquid?

If a squid is squirting inky liquid, what will the squid want to do next?

If a squirrel gets attacked, will the squirrel squirt an inky, black liquid at its attacker?

If a quick squirrel, quacking duck or squirmy squid attacks you, will you squirt inky liquid?

Can you use the number of words and the endings of the words to say what kind of family a list is?

quick	squirrel	squid	quip	quill	quilt	quilt	quit
quicker	squirrels	squid	quips	quills	quilts	quilts	quits
quickest						quilting	quitting
						quilted	quit

query	query	squint	quiz	quiz	squirt	squirt
queries	queries	squints	quizzes	quizzes	squirts	squirts
	querying	squinting		quizzing		squirting
	queried	squinted		quizzed		squirted

quirky	squirmy	squirm	squiggle	quest
quirkier	squirmier	squirms	squiggles	quests
quirkiest	squirmiest	squirming		
		squirmed		

Write a new page of noun phrases into your Notebook. Start each phrase with an article from pg. 86.

Use an *adjective* or <u>noun</u> from above in every phrase as you write your new noun phrases.

Then say one sentence that starts with each phrase. Try to use some verbs from the lists on this page.

You may want to take turns with your Reader, or you may want to say all the sentences yourself.

Can you use the verb "chased" to connect any 2 of the noun phrases below in 1 sentence?

Can you think of any other verbs or phrases that could connect any 2 of the phrases below?

our *squirmy* <u>kids</u>

        the *quickest* <u>squirrel</u>

               six *quacking, squirming* <u>ducks</u>

                   one *happy* <u>squid</u>, two *fast* <u>squid</u>, three *angry* <u>squid</u>

                       two *quirky quick* <u>quizzes</u>

Our *squirmy* <u>kids</u> ran after a *squinting* <u>squirrel</u>, but the <u>squirrel</u> was quicker than our <u>kids</u>.

The sentences on this page are correct.

Use this page to study which of 2 words (on that line) that end with "__" needs an "s" in the "__."

On pg. 102, you will decide which blank in each line needs an "s" for the sentence(s) to make sense.

Can you say which words with blanks on the end are nouns and which are verbs?

Many ducks quack__; but if it is just one duck, the one duck quack<u>s</u>_.

One squirrel run<u>s</u>_; but if it is many squirrels, the many squirrels run__.

One squirrel__ is called a squirrel. Six squirrel<u>s</u>_ are called several squirrels.

One dog is called a dog__. Seven dogs are called several dog<u>s</u>_ or many dogs.

One cat__ is called a cat. Ten cat<u>s</u>_ are called many cats.

One squid is called a squid. Eleven squid are called many squid.

Nouns use an "s" on the end to say "more than one."

Nouns that mean "more than one" are called "plural."

Some plural nouns do not use an "s" at the end.

"Squid" is one of the plural nouns with no "s" at the end.

In the first sentence below, which word tells you the first "squid" is a single squid?

Which word tells you the second "squid" is plural? Both words are articles.

A squid squirt<u>s</u>_ an inky liquid, but many squid squirt__ inky liquid.

Many dogs eat__; but a dog eat<u>s</u>_ . I eat. You eat. We eat. But he eats and she eats.

I sing. You sing. We sing. They sing. He sings. She sing<u>s</u>_. But they both sing__.

I sit. You sit. We sit. They sit. He sit<u>s</u>_, and she sits, but the three of us sit__.

I drink. You drink. We drink. They drink. He drinks. She drink<u>s</u>_. They all drink__.

Use S-verbs with a singular (S-less) noun. Use S-less root verbs with plural (S-ending) nouns.

Use this page the same way you used the last page, to study which blanks ("__") need an "s".

I squirm. You squirm__. We squirm. They squirm. He squirms. She squirm<u>s</u>.

That squirrel squirm<u>s</u>. The other squirrels squirm__.

A squirrel__ squirms. Many squirrel<u>s</u> squirm. Squirmy squirrels squirm the most.

Any fully alive squid is squirmier than even the squirmiest squirrel.

I squirt__. You squirt. We squirt. She squirts. He squirt<u>s</u>. What do they squirt?

A squid squirt<u>s</u> inky liquid. All squid squirt__ inky liquid.

Anyone that thinks is a thinker. Any thinker thinks.

Anyone that drums is a drummer. Any drummer drums.

Anyone that plays is a player. Any player plays. Can you play today?

Any squirter squirt<u>s</u>. Anyone that squirts is a squirter. All squirters squirt__.

Any squirmer squirm<u>s</u>. Anyone that squirms is a squirmer. All squirmers squirm__.

Any singer sing<u>s</u>. Anyone that sings is a singer. All singers sing__.

Ten finger<u>s</u> finger the clarinet in our band. That is one clarinetist__.

Four hands play__ the trumpets in our band. That is two trumpeter<u>s</u>.

Twenty fingers drum__ four drumstick<u>s</u> on 6 drums in the four hands of two drummers.

Ten hands play nine instrument<u>s</u>, one clarinet__, two trumpets and six drums.

That squid under the rock squirt<u>s</u> the inky liquid that all squid squirt__ when attacked.

Will a squirrel squirt__ an inky, black liquid if the squirrel get<u>s</u> attacked?

I have one pair__ of flip-flops. That is two flip-flop<u>s</u>.

I have two pairs of flippers. That is four flippers.

I have three pairs of slippers. That is six slippers.

I have four sneakers. That is two pairs of sneakers.

I have two shoes. That is one pair of shoes.

For each line below, decide which blank needs an "s" for that sentence to make sense.

You can check your choice by looking at the same sentence in the sentences on the two prior pages.

Many ducks quack__; but if it is just one duck, the one duck quack__.

One squirrel run__; but if it is many squirrels, the many squirrels run__.

Many dogs eat__; but a dog eat__. I eat. You eat. We eat. Bet he eats and she eats.

I squirm. You squirm__. We squirm. They squirm. He squirms. She squirm__.

That squirrel squirm__. The other squirrels squirm__.

A squirrel__ squirms. Many squirrel__ squirm.

Any squirter squirt__. Anyone that squirts is a squirter. All squirters squirt__.

Any squirmer squirm__. Anyone that squirms is a squirmer. All squirmers squirm__.

Any singer sing__. Anyone that sings is a singer. All singers sing__.

I squirt__. You squirt. We squirt. She squirts. He squirt__. They squirt.

A squid squirt__ inky liquid. All squid squirt__ inky liquid.

That squid under the rock squirt__ the inky liquid that all squid squirt__ when attacked.

Will a squirrel squirt__ an inky, black liquid if the squirrel get__ attacked?

Ten finger__ finger the clarinet in our band. That is one clarinetist__.

Four hands play__ the trumpets in our band. That is two trumpeter__.

Twenty fingers drum__ four drumstick__ on 6 drums in the four hands of two drummers.

Ten hands play nine instrument__, one clarinet__, two trumpets and six drums.

I have one pair__ of flip-flops. That is two flip-flop__.

Can you tell a longer story by adding to any of these stories?

One sentence in each group below needs an "s" in it to make sense.

Which blank needs an "s" for its sentence to make sense ?

He swims when he can swim.

Jim swim__ when Jim can swim__ .

I swim when I can swim.

What wags on my dog if she is happy?

That dog__ wag__ his tail if he is happy.

Dogs wag their tails when they are happy.

Wally's mom will not wax his floor after he mops it.

Wally will wax his floor__ after he mop__ it.

Wally's dog will not wax his floor, nor will she mop it.

I wait every day for the bus.

Walter wait__ every day__ for the bus.

We wait every day for the bus, and they wait every day also.

Georgia and George give funny wax wigs away at a mall on Saturdays.

Georgia give__ away the funniest wax wigs at the mall__ .

George gives away the sturdiest wax wigs at the mall.

All twenty dragons swim every Sunday.

That dragon__ swim__ on Saturdays, too.

That dog swims, too, whenever she can.

Check your choices on page 184.

Every verb family has 4 verbs that mean the same kind of action in 4 sets of situations.

Look at the names of the 4 forms of a verb.

Verb Form	Sets of Situations
Root Verb	(any plural noun phrase) I you we they Henry and Babe Jack and Jill
S-Verb	(any singular noun phrase) she he Jessica Sandy Markell Cecilia Raymond
ING-Verb	could be ___ing would be ___ing should be ___ing am ___ing are ___ing is ___ing were ___ing hate ___ing likes ___ing hated ___ing liked ___ing
Past Verb	last week last month last year yesterday a minute ago a second ago

"Past Verb" is short to say and write, but think of "Past Verb" as "before now" when you say it.

Here are the 2 Forms of a noun.

Noun Form		Sets of Situations	Examples	
Root Noun	is a **"Singular Noun"**	one of it	fly	ball
S-Noun	is a **"Plural Noun"**	more than one of it	flies	balls

ING-Verbs and Past Verbs work with both Noun Forms, singular and plural.

If you do not need an ING or Past Verb,

use an S-Verb for a Root Noun,

use a Root Verb for a (plural) S-Noun.

Root Nouns never work with Root Verbs. S-Nouns never work with S-Verbs.

Examples

Some birds swim. The dogs jump. Cats purr. Whistlers whistle. Even little frogs jump.
What bird swims? The dog jumps. My cat purrs. Which whistle whistles? My frog jumps.

Many things sing.   Many bees sting.   Many singers sing.
I wonder.   You help.   We floss.   They giggle.   Mark and Marc run more than I do.

That thing sings.   One bee stings.   One singer sings.   Who sings lullabies?
She swims every morning and he swims every evening.   Who swims here daily?
Jessica spells well.   Sandy studies spelling.   Martin says Cecilia spells faster than Mary.

You could be helping.   I would be dancing.   We should be working.
I am helping. We are dancing. She is working. He was working when we were working.
We hate sitting still. He likes talking.   They liked walking. We talk about walking too.

Last week I walked. We talked last month. She sang at a concert last year.
Yesterday I swam in a river. Yesterday my sister swam, then she fished in a lake.
The banjo player played for an hour, two hours ago. A drummer rang bells with sticks.

Can you underline the endings of every verb on this page? Which Verb Form has no ending?

Underline the whole word when you see a root verb. Use page 185 to check your answers.

For the 3 Past Verbs that don't have an ED, underline the letter that is not in that family's root word.

Can you read each short story on this page on your own?

Count the words you need help with the 1ˢᵗ time. Re-read the story and count again. Do it a 3ʳᵈ time.

Did you need help with fewer words each time you re-read the story?

Frances danced a <u>fancy</u> dance, then Nancy danced a <u>fancier</u> dance than Frances.

But they only had two legs after all, and Prancer had four.

So Prancer pranced the <u>fanciest</u> dance of all the dancers to win the Fancy Dance Contest.

Nancy danced <u>fancier</u> than Frances. The judges said Prancer danced <u>fanciest</u>, prancing.

"What do they expect, with Prancer having four legs?" objected Frances and Nancy.

I always have one box of pencils in my desk.

But sometimes I have more, so I put the <u>excess</u> pencils on top of my desk in a cup.

The <u>excess</u> pencils in the cup are extras for anyone who needs a pencil.

When Cecilia said she had an "accent" when she was in the gym, I was puzzled.

Cecilia always has an accent. Then she said, "the accent hurt my ankle."

I told her, "It was an 'accident' when you hurt your ankle. You hurt it in an 'accident.' "

We both giggled at her mistake. "It takes a lot of mistakes to learn a language," she said.

Many wolves were gathered at the edge of the <u>long</u> bridge, by the <u>huge</u> fence.

The wolves were interested in the many, many mice living under the bridge and the fence.

It is a mystery that something so <u>big</u> and <u>heavy</u> can fly in the sky! And it flies so <u>high</u>.

<u>Heavy</u> things fall. Birds fly. Birds are not <u>heavy</u>, and birds are not <u>big</u>. <u>Heavy</u> things fall.

Birds that fly are not <u>heavy</u>. Flies are not <u>big</u> or <u>heavy</u>. Butterflies are not <u>big</u> or <u>heavy</u>.

Critters that fly are not <u>big</u> and they are not <u>heavy</u>. Critters that are <u>big</u> or <u>heavy</u> do not fly.

But the <u>big</u>, <u>heavy</u>, <u>metal</u> things akin to a <u>giant</u> bird can fly so <u>fast</u>. It is a mystery to me!

The <u>mystery</u> thing's <u>stiff</u>, <u>heavy</u>, <u>strong</u>, <u>metal</u> wings do not flap in the wind.

Can you say the name of the <u>mysterious</u> <u>bird-like</u> <u>metal</u> thing flying across the sky?

Have you ever been in a <u>big</u>, <u>heavy</u>, <u>bird-like</u> <u>metal</u> thing flying across the sky?

Was it the verbs, the nouns, or the adjectives that we underlined on this page?

Reader reads each sentence on page 106 while Learner looks at this page.

Learner changes Root_ Verbs, Root_ Adjectives and Root_ Nouns to use a correct ending.

Cross out the Root Word's final letter first if you need to. Spell any endings diagonally above the "_."

Frances dance**d** a fancy_ dance_, then Nancy dance**d** a fancy**ier** dance_ than Frances.

But they only had two leg_ after all, and Prancer had four.

Prancer prance_ the fancy_ dance_ of all the dancer_ to win_ the Fancy Dance Contest.

Nancy dance_ fancy_ than Frances. The judge_ said Prancer dance_ fancy_, prance_.

"What do they expect_, with Prancer have_ four leg_?" object_ Frances and Nancy.

I always have_ one box of pencil_ in my desk_.

But sometimes I have_ more, so I put the excess_ pencil_ on top of my desk_ in a cup_.

The excess_ pencil_ in the cup_ are extra_ for anyone who need_ a pencil.

When Cecilia say_ she had an "accent_" when she was in the gym_, I was puzzle_.

Cecilia always had an accent_. Then she say_, "the accent_ hurt_ my ankle_."

"It was an 'accident_' when you hurt_ your ankle_. You hurt_ it in an 'accident_.' "

We giggle_ at her mistake_. "It take_ a lot of mistake_ to learn_ a language_," she say_.

It is a mystery_ that something_ so big_ and heavy_ can fly_ in the sky_!

Heavy_ thing_ fall_. Bird_ fly_. Bird_ are not heavy_, and bird_ are not big_.

Bird_ that fly_ are not heavy_. Butterfly_ and fly_ are not big_ or heavy_.

Critter_ that fly_ are not big_ and they are not heavy_. Big_, heavy_ critter_ do_ not fly_.

But the big_, heavy_, metal_ thing_ akin to a giant_ bird_ can fly_. It is a mystery_ to me!

The mystery_ thing_'s stiff_, heavy_, strong_, metal_ wing_ do_ not flap_ in the wind_.

Can you say_ the name_ of the mysterious bird-like metal thing_ fly_ across the sky_?

Have you ever been in a big_ heavy_ bird-like metal thing_ fly_ across the sky?

Can you underline each adjective in these stories the way we did on the previous page?

What page can you use to check the words you chose to underline as adjectives?

We call this   **Blank Families' Stories.**

You will need at least 2 blank pages of paper and pencils.

Pick a story that uses more than 2 words from any one verb family or adjective family.

>   Stories that have 2 or 3 such families are even better for this game.

Read the story, then re-read it.

As you re-read it, underline all the words from all the families you chose that story for.

List all the words in those families on your 1st blank paper.

>   List all the words from those families that you underlined.

>   List all the words from those families that are not in the story.

Now copy the story on the 2nd blank paper.

As you copy the story on the 2nd blank paper, replace the underlined words with empty blank lines.

Put them away in a safe place for a week, where you don't look at them, but know where they are.

>   Staple or paper clip your 2 pages together before you put them away.

>   If it is easy to get 3 copies of each page made on a copy machine, that is even better.

After a week, you have a practice page (or copies) you can use several times if you write lightly.

That is   **Blank Families' Stories.**

We call this   **Trading Places**.

Pick a story that uses 2 or more words from any verb family or adjective family.

Pick 2 words from the same family that both occur in the story you picked.

As you read the story the 1st time, circle the 2 words wherever they occur in the story.

Above each of your 2 words, write the other.

As you read the story a 2nd time, pretend each word has replaced the other, wherever either occurs.

Read the story aloud, using the substitute verbs.

Do the sentences make sense?   No.

Change the words you need to change for each sentence to make sense.

Write any new words lightly in pencil, with a mark to show where they go.

Circle any words or phrases you want to delete (subtract) from a sentence.

Read the story a 3rd time, aloud, using all the changes you chose to make.

That is   **Trading Places**.

Celebrate finishing Chapter 4 by reading any or all of the following books.

Night Cat   Margaret Beames, Sue Hitchcock
Duck in the Truck   Jez Alborough
Bad Boys   Margie Palatini, Henry Cole
Courage   Bernard Waber
Richard Scarry's Best Word Book Ever   Richard Scarry

You can color these letters you have learned.

Wall

Quack

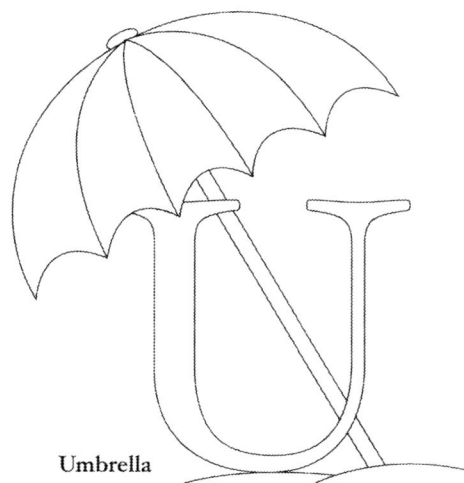

Umbrella

Chapter 5

Goals

Meet and practice Silent E Teams.
(pp. 113 - 139)
See verb families, noun families, & adjective families side-by-side, and know which are which.
(pp. 113 - 123 , 126 , 129 - 137)

Here are some Practice Suggestions you may want to try.

Pick any verb family from any page of any Chapter.

Turn to page 53 in Chapter 2.

Practice using the 4 verbs of the verb family you picked in the sample sentences on page 53.

Take turns adding a few sentences at a time to put them together into stories.

Next, pick 2 verb families to mix together in your sentences and stories. Then pick 3.

Pick a row of verb familes. Pick 1 of the 4 kinds of verbs: root, S-ending, ING-ending, or past verb.

All the verbs of that kind in that row of verb families are on the same line of print.

Use the whole line of verbs, one after another, to make sentences.

After you use the 1st verb in a sentence, try to use the next verb in the same spot in that sentence.

Decide whether the sentence you made by substituting the new verb for the prior verb makes sense.

Then make another sentence for the second verb.

Repeat the process for every pair of consecutive verbs.

PRACTICE CALENDAR
CHAPTER 5

DAY & DATE	TIME	PAGE	NOTES, COMMENTS

You have practiced 3 kinds of word families: adjective, noun, and verb.

Can you draw a line to separate
          the families with A's Name Sound from the families with A's Short Sound?

Read each word family after your Reader reads it to you.

Draw the line after you have read all the families.

late	great	safe		gate	games	date
later	greater	safer		gates	games	dates
latest	greatest	safest	pace	space	face	lace
			paces	spaces	faces	laces
pale	tame	sage		scale	sail	tail	nail
paler	tamer	sager		scales	sails	tails	nails
palest	tamest	sagest	rate	sale	tale	cage
			rates	sales	tales	cages
sad	glad	mad		tad	pad	bat
sadder	gladder	madder		tads	pads	bats
saddest	gladdest	maddest	fan	gap	map	man
			fans	gaps	maps	men

pass	plan	can	clap	tap	stack	have
passes	plans	cans	claps	taps	stacks	has
passing	planning	canning	clapping	tapping	stacking	having
passed	planned	canned	clapped	tapped	stacked	had

Make a list of noun phrases in your Notebook using adjectives and nouns from this and other pages.

Which *adjective* families make sense with which <u>noun</u> families?

          Can a <u>gate</u> be *glad*? Can a <u>game</u> be *great*? Can <u>bats</u> be *safer*? Can <u>cages</u> be *madder*?

Can you make two noun phrases into a sentence by using a verb that makes sense between them?

Use the directions from this page to do the next two pages in the same way.

name	tame	blame	flame	cram	ram	slam
names	tames	blames	flames	crams	rams	slams
naming	taming	blaming	flaming	cramming	ramming	slamming
named	tamed	blamed	flamed	crammed	rammed	slammed

bake	fake	take	shake	pack	lack	track
bakes	fakes	takes	shakes	packs	lacks	tracks
baking	faking	taking	shaking	packing	lacking	tracking
baked	faked	took	shook	packed	lacked	tracked

inflate	grate	rate	state	skate	pat	bat
inflates	grates	rates	states	skates	pats	bats
inflating	grating	rating	stating	skating	patting	batting
inflated	grated	rated	stated	skated	patted	batted

tape	escape	scrape	trap	snap	clap	happen
tapes	escapes	scrapes	traps	snaps	claps	happens
taping	escaping	scraping	trapping	snapping	clapping	happening
taped	escaped	scraped	trapped	snapped	clapped	happened

fade	trade	wade	shade	pad	add
fades	trades	wades	shades	pads	adds
fading	trading	wading	shading	padding	adding
faded	traded	waded	shaded	padded	added

What clues did you use to decide which root words had Name Sounds and which had Short Sounds?

We've underlined the letter team that spells A's Name Sound in some words above.

Can you do the same for the other words on this page?

Can you tell a Verb Family Story using any of the verb families on this page?

Circle the 3 verb families on this page that have neither A's Name Sound nor A's Short Sound.

Draw a line between verb families that have A's Name Sound & those that have A's Short Sound.

ail	fail	trail	hail	call	stall	fall
ails	fails	trails	hails	calls	stalls	falls
ailing	failing	trailing	hailing	calling	stalling	falling
ailed	failed	trailed	hailed	called	stalled	fell

wake	break	brake	make	stack	crack	lack
wakes	breaks	brakes	makes	stacks	cracks	lacks
waking	breaking	braking	making	stacking	cracking	lacking
woke	broke	braked	made	stacked	cracked	lacked

rain	train	strain	stain	gain	drain	fan
rains	trains	strains	stains	gains	drains	fans
raining	training	straining	staining	gaining	draining	fanning
rained	trained	strained	stained	gained	drained	fanned

gaze	amaze	race	trace	face	pass	jazz
gazes	amazes	races	traces	faces	passes	jazzes
gazing	amazing	racing	tracing	facing	passing	jazzing
gazed	amazed	raced	traced	faces	passed	jazzed

save	have	gab	grab	dab	nab	blab
saves	has	gabs	grabs	dabs	nabs	blabs
saving	having	gabbing	grabbing	dabbing	nabbing	blabbing
saved	had	gabbed	grabbed	dabbed	nabbed	blabbed

Can you find all five of the past verbs that do not spell "by the plan?"

Can you find the one S-ending verb that does not spell "by the plan?"

Below are some examples of root words, adjectives, nouns and verbs, that end with a Silent E Team.

Do you want to read these root words yourself, or do you want your Reader to read them to you first?

| cane | late | hope | note | fuse | poke | date | tale | cube |

Compare the words in each pair below, to see and hear the difference adding a Silent E makes.

| can | hat | hop | not | fuss | wok | rat | tall | cub |
| cane | hate | hope | note | fuse | woke | rate | tale | cube |

Compare the verb families below.

Draw a line between families of root words ending with Silent E & root words ending with a consonant.

pile	style	smile	fill	spill	refill	will
piles	styles	smiles	fills	spills	refills	wills
piling	styling	smiling	filling	spilling	refilling	willing
piled	styled	smiled	filled	spilled	refilled	willed

bite	hide	write	type	hit	fit	sit
bites	hides	writes	types	hits	fits	sits
biting	hiding	writing	typing	hitting	fitting	sitting
bit	hid	wrote	typed	hit	fit	sat

rise	whine	shine	rhyme	dim	spin	win
rises	whines	shines	rhymes	dims	spins	wins
rising	whining	shining	rhyming	dimming	spinning	winning
rose	whined	shined	rhymed	dimmed	spun	won

Is your line also a line between families that have I's Name Sound & those that have I's Short Sound?

Did you see this yourself before we asked you?

Did you remember to read Y in the middle of a word as if it were an I ?

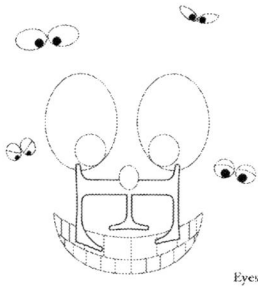

A Silent E team needs 3 parts to be a Silent E team:

a Silent E ending,

only one prior consonant, immediately before the Silent E ending,

only one prior vowel, immediately before the one consonant.

In the row of root words below, the 1 prior consonant is underlined, the 1 prior vowel is in *italics*.

ca*n*e   la*t*e   ho*p*e   no*t*e   tu*b*e   po*k*e   da*t*e   ta*l*e   cu*b*e

If a word ends with a Silent E team, then the 1 vowel prior to the 1 consonant spells its Name Sound.

So far we have been telling you how Silent E teams can end a **Root Word.**

Root words are part of larger verb, adjective or noun families.

hope	mope	lope	code	joke	close	place
hopes	mopes	lopes	codes	jokes	closes	places
hoping	moping	loping	coding	joking	closing	placing
hoped	moped	loped	coded	joked	closed	placed

tame	ripe	late	cute	close	nice
tamer	riper	later	cuter	closer	nicer
tamest	ripest	latest	cutest	closest	nicest

cane	race	rose	rope	spine	pile	rule
canes	races	roses	ropes	spines	piles	rules

In families whose root words end with a Silent E Team, spelling a Name Sound,

do all the words in the family have that Name Sound?

All the words in the whole family have the same vowel sound as the root word.

Some root words look like they have a Silent E team in the word, but do not.   have   give   love

Draw a line between families with Name Sounds and those with Short Sounds,

pit	ride	stripe	kite	size	prize	smile
pits	rides	stripes	kites	sizes	prizes	smiles

whim	hill	rip	side	line	style	rhyme
whims	hills	rips	sides	lines	styles	rhymes

snack	bag	bat	skate	trade	shape	grape	spice	space	eye
snacks	bags	bats	skates	trades	shapes	grapes	spices	spaces	eyes

top	crop	hop	rock	poke	hope	hose	rose	nose
tops	crops	hops	rocks	pokes	hopes	hoses	roses	noses

Use <u>1</u> consonant to connect a prior name-sound vowel to an ER or EST ending.

tame	late	stale	close	wide	wise	nice
tamer	later	staler	closer	wider	wiser	nicer
tamest	latest	stalest	closest	widest	wisest	nicest

Use <u>2</u> consonants to separate a prior short-sound vowel from an ER or EST ending.

thin	grim	glad	sad	mad	big
thinner	grimmer	gladder	sadder	madder	bigger
thinnest	grimmest	gladdest	saddest	maddest	biggest

Why do we double the root word's final consonant before we add an ER or EST ending?

So that "thinner" and "thinnest" will not look like "thiner" and "thinest,"   like Silent E Teams.

In most word families, all the words keep the sounds of the root word.

Short vowel sounds need 2 consonants between a single prior vowel and ER, EST, ING or ED.

Two consonants between a prior vowel and those endings tells you this is not a Silent E Team.

In these families, we double a consonant to not look like a word from a Silent E Team family.

dim	sad	glad	mad	slim	wet	hot
dimmer	sadder	gladder	madder	slimmer	wetter	hotter
dimmest	saddest	gladdest	maddest	slimmest	wettest	hottest

clap	sled	slip	strum	drum	hum	stun
claps	sleds	slips	strums	drums	hums	stuns
clapping	sledding	slipping	strumming	drumming	humming	stunning
clapped	sledded	slipped	strummed	drummed	hummed	stunned

grip	spot	stop	skim	skip	grin	rub
grips	spots	stops	skims	skips	grins	rubs
gripping	spotting	stopping	skimming	skipping	grinning	rubbing
gripped	spotted	stopped	skimmed	skipped	grinned	rubbed

Compare the family spelling plan below to the family spelling plan above.

place	race	hose	close	joke	hike	like
places	races	hoses	closes	jokes	hikes	likes
placing	racing	hosing	closing	joking	hiking	liking
placed	raced	hosed	closed	joked	hiked	liked

How do the endings of the root verbs below differ from both kinds of root verb endings above?

jump	sprint	fuss	kick	spill	fill	end
jumps	sprints	fusses	kicks	spills	fills	ends
jumping	sprinting	fussing	kicking	spilling	filling	ending
jumped	sprinted	fussed	kicked	spilled	filled	ended

<u>Root verbs that end with 2 consonants</u> don't need a consonant added before ING or ED endings.

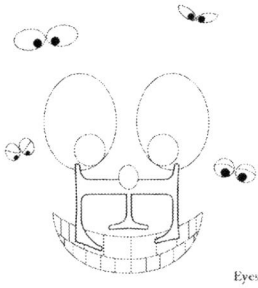

A Silent E team needs 3 parts to be a Silent E team:

a Silent E ending,

only **one** **prior** consonant, immediately before the silent E ending,

only **one** **prior** vowel, immediately before the one consonant.

A root word that has the last 2 of those 3 parts, but no Silent E at the end, is not a Silent E Team.

dim   thin   flat   drag   step   red   log

When we add adjective endings ER or EST,   or we add verb endings ING or ED,

the last two words in the adjective and verb families will look exactly like

the adjective and verb endings for root words with Silent E Teams look.

dim	drag	hop	thin	flat	red
dims	drags	hops	*thiner*	*flater*	*reder*
diming	*draging*	*hoping*	*thinest*	*flatest*	*redest*
dimed	*draged*	*hoped*			

If the last two words in each family look wrong to you, you are starting to be a speller just by reading.

Adding an ending that works like a Silent E ending   to a root word that ends vowel-consonant,

gives a result that looks like a Silent E Team at work, spelling a prior vowel's Name Sound.

So, if we **don't** want a Name Sound we double the consonant so it **won't** look like a Silent E Team.

The same adjective and verb families spell a prior vowel short sound by using **2** prior consonants.

dim	drag	hop	thin	flat	red
dims	drags	hops	thinner	flatter	redder
dimming	dragging	hopping	thinnest	flattest	reddest
dimmed	dragged	hopped			

Re-read the last page before filling in the blanks in the verb and adjective families below.

Remember you are trying to keep the same Short Sound or Name Sound for all the verbs in the family.

How do we use the 1 or 2 consonants that go in each blank to do that?

strum	drip	spot	scan	rub	sled
stru___s	dri___s	spo___s	sca___s	ru___s	sle___s
stru___ing	dri___ing	spo___ing	sca___ing	ru___ing	sle___ing
stru___ed	dri___ed	spo___ed	sca___ed	ru___ed	sle___ed

stroke	skate	tame	mine	bake	hope	close
stro___es	ska___es	ta___es	mi___es	ba___es	ho___es	clo___es
stro___ing	ska___ing	ta___ing	mi___ing	ba___ing	ho___ing	clo___ing
stro___ed	ska___ed	ta___ed	mi___ed	ba___ed	ho___ed	clo___ed

stride	ride	skim	can	bat	kick	clip
stri___es	ri___es	ski___s	ca___s	ba___s	ki___s	cli___s
stri___ing	ri___ing	ski___ing	ca___ing	ba___ing	ki___ing	cli___ing
stro___e	ro___e	ski___ed	ca___ed	ba___ed	ki___ed	cli___ed

cute	late	tame	dim	hot	stiff	dull
cu___er	la___er	ta___er	di___er	ho___er	sti___er	du___er
cu___est	la___est	ta___est	di___est	ho___est	sti___est	du___est

nice	thick	fake	huge	big	quick	sad
ni___er	thi___er	fa___er	hu___er	bi___er	qui___er	sa___er
ni___est	thi___est	fa___est	hu___est	bi___est	qui___est	sa___est

Which verb ending always has the same number of prior consonants that its root verb has? ___
Use page 186 to check your spelling choices on this page.

Which of the 5 rows have verb families? Which rows have adjective families?
Which are easier for you to think of: Verb Family Stories or Adjective Family Stories?

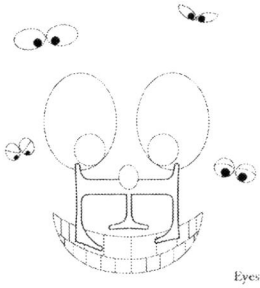

A Silent E Team needs 3 parts to be a Silent E Team:

a Silent E ending,

only one prior consonant, immediately before the Silent E ending,

only one prior vowel, immediately before the one consonant.

But not if the prior consonant is V and the prior vowel is O !

If V is the consonant between a prior vowel and a final Silent E, then you need to recognize the word!

It will be helpful to you to quickly re-read pages 27-29 from Chapter 1, before continuing this page.

Compare the families on the left side to the families on the right side.

stove	grove		cover	shovel	glove	dove	oven
stoves	groves		covers	shovels	gloves	doves	ovens

strive	dive	drive	cover	shovel	shove	love
strives	dives	drives	covers	shovels	shoves	loves
striving	diving	driving	covering	shoveling	shoving	loving
strove	dove	drove	covered	shoveled	shoved	loved

clove	clover		move	prove	improve	disprove
cloves	clovers		moves	proves	improves	disproves
			moving	proving	improving	disproving
			moved	proved	improved	disproved

Root words that end with O as the prior vowel and V as the prior consonant, OVE, are unusual.

With words that have OVE, you just have to recognize the word and its family to read the vowel sound.

You do the same with the families of these 3 root verbs: have   give   live

I have gloves that I cover my hands with whenever I use a shovel to move dirt.

Using gloves when shoveling dirt improves the way your hands feel after you're done.

Can you read all the different vowel sounds that are followed by V in this story?

Before reading the story, underline all the words that have a V between a vowel and an E.

When Dave and I drive up to a house, pull to a stop, and park, we always hear the kids who live there yelling, "Here are the movers."

And Dave always says, "They're the ones moving, not me. I'm living in the same house I lived in when I was a kid, the same house my dad built."

Dave loves to tell the kids that they are the movers, not Dave and I. But the kids call us the movers anyway. Some kids call us home movers, but we don't move homes or houses, we move everything that people keep in them.

We put our gloves on and put the people's belongings in the back of our big truck.

We start with the big, heavy things, like ovens, stoves, dishwashers and cabinets.

Then we cover everything with thick, soft covers.

Then we add lots of smaller, heavy things, like boxes of books, dishes or tools.

We shove everything as close together as we can get it, so it can't move or slide in the back of the truck later, when we drive the truck. If there is no space between things, the things have no room to move around and bump into each other. If nothing can move or bump, nothing can break. We hope. We cover everything with soft cloth just in case.

Can you colorize all the vowel sounds in the words above that you underlined?
Write the verb families of any verbs in the story that you underlined.

_____   _____   _____   _____   _____   _____   _____

_____   _____   _____   _____   _____   _____   _____

_____   _____   _____   _____   _____   _____   _____

_____   _____   _____   _____   _____   _____   _____

Did you remember the sounds spelled by O in these families, or did you use context to read them?

You can use page 193 to check the work you did on this page.

I was dozing in the green grass, on a folded old gold blanket I had seen in an old trunk.

My older brother was holding a hose, watering the grass across our yard, a long way away.

As I dozed off I began to dream. I dreamt I was at the beach sleeping and a wave hit me.

I dreamt my older brother saved me from a wave by pulling me onto the beach to safety.

Now my brother was everybody's hero for saving my life by pulling me out of the water.

That was my dream. I was glad to be saved. I was freezing cold from the cold water.

Then I woke up. I saw my older brother standing over me spraying me with the hose.

I know a poet who likes to write rhymes. She writes rhymes about everything she likes.

She even writes rhymes about things she does not like. She puts rhythms into her rhymes.

She just likes to write rhymes all the time. This poet's name is Lucy. She likes kids a lot.

Even more than writing rhythmic rhymes, Lucy likes to receive rhymes as gifts.

She likes her gift rhymes to be given to her wrapped in fancy paper with ribbons.

She says getting her gift rhymes wrapped in fancy paper and ribbons proves they are gifts.

She likes getting gift rhymes best when the gift rhymes are a surprise.

Actually, she is very picky. The gift rhymes have to be a completely unexpected surprise.

That was a lot to expect from her friends and family, when all knew she expected rhymes.

How could they surprise her with what she expected?

Besides, none of them ever wrote rhymes at all, except when they wrote a rhyme for her.

They knew the poet often liked funny rhymes. They knew they only wrote boring rhymes.

It was a problem for the poet and a problem for her friends, who wanted her to be happy.

Then the poet had an idea as she was supervising a game of hide-and-seek one evening.

Now, whenever a child is visiting the poet, the poet gives the child a rhyme to hide.

The child takes the rhyme to another place to wrap the rhyme in fancy paper and ribbon.

The children love hiding rhymes in all the secret hiding places all over the poet's home.

The poet does not look for the rhymes, but she finds them from time to time, by surprise.

The children hide the rhymes so well that most of her rhymes seem new as she reads them.

Some of the blanks we put in these stories need a single consonant, some need a double consonant.

Why do the spaces that need a double consonant need two consonants instead of one?

What kind of vowel sound is before the spaces with 2 consonants, a Short Sound or a Name Sound?

What kind of vowel sound is usually before the spaces with 1 consonant followed by a final Silent E,

a Short Sound or a Name Sound?

I was dozing in the green grass, on a folded old gold blanket I had seen in the trunk.

My older brother was using a hose to water the gra___ acro___ the yard, a long way away.

As I do___ed off I began to dream. I dreamt I was at the beach sleeping and a wave hit me.

I dreamt my older brother sa___ed me from a wave by pulling me onto the beach to safety.

Now my brother was everybody's hero for saving my li___e by pulling me out of the water.

That was my dream. I was glad to be sa___ed. I was freezing cold from the cold water.

Then I wo___e up. I saw my older brother standing o___er me spraying me with the ho___e.

The poet likes her gift rhymes to be gi___en to her wra___ed in fancy paper with ribbons.

She says getting her gift rhymes wrapped in fancy paper and ribbons proves they are gifts.

She li___es ge___ing gift rhy___es best when the gift rhymes are a comple___e surprise.

Actually, she is very picky. The gift rhymes have to be a completely unexpected surpri___e.

Surprise was a lot to expect from friends and family when she knew she expected rhymes.

How could they surpri___e her when she knew they knew rhy___es was the gift she wanted?

Also, none of them ever wro___e rhymes except when they wrote a rhy___e, badly, for her.

They knew the poet often li___ed fu___y rhy___es. They knew they wro___e boring rhymes.

They knew the poet expected rhy___es from her friends, so how could they surpri___e her.

It was a problem for the poet and a problem for her friends, who wanted her to be ha___y.

Then the poet had an idea as she was supervising a ga___e of hi___e-and-seek one e___ening.

Now whene___er a child is visiting the poet, the poet gi___es the child a rhyme to hi___e.

The children love hiding rhymes in all the secret hiding places all o___er the poet's home.

The poet does not look for the rhy___es, but she finds them from ti___e to time, by surprise.

The children hi___e the rhy___es so well that most of her rhymes seem new as she reads them.

Y can team with **1** vowel prior to **1** consonant prior to a **final** Y to spell the vowel's **Name Sound**.

Y endings work like Silent E endings to help a prior vowel spell its Name Sound.

Do you wish to read these families before your Reader reads them, or after?

funny	happy	sunny	merry	silly	lazy	tiny
funnier	happier	sunnier	merrier	sillier	lazier	tinier
funniest	happiest	sunniest	merriest	silliest	laziest	tiniest

ferry	bury	carry	marry	rely	deny	defy
ferries	buries	carries	marries	relies	denies	defies
ferrying	burying	carrying	marrying	relying	denying	defying
ferried	buried	carried	married	relied	denied	defied

messy	sunny	foggy	drippy	cozy	rosy	holy
messier	sunnier	foggier	drippier	cozier	rosier	holier
messiest	sunniest	foggiest	drippiest	coziest	rosiest	holiest

body	berry	penny	pony	lady	duty	ruby
bodies	berries	pennies	ponies	ladies	duties	rubies

Are you still drawing a line separating families with Short Vowel Sounds from Name Vowel Sounds?

Did you notice what happened to the Y as we added each ending in the families above?

What letter does a Y ending change to when any ending with E is added to the root word?   _____

For which verb ending did Y not change to I before we added the ending?   _____

For which verb & noun ending did we add E as part of the ending, after the Y changed to I?   _____

Y can team with **one** vowel prior to **one** consonant prior to a **final** Y to spell the vowel's **Name** Sound.

Adjective, noun and verb endings need 2 consonants between Y and a prior vowel's Short Sound.

Always notice how many consonants are between <u>any</u> family endings and a prior vowel.

My Aunt Ruby just loves gloves.

She has fancy gloves and funny gloves, colorful gloves and ugly or silly gloves.

Just when you think you have seen all her gloves, she opens a box full of other gloves.

The other gloves are sillier and uglier and funnier and fancier than all those first gloves.

But just when you think you have seen all her gloves, she opens another boxful of gloves.

This next boxful is even sillier and fancier and uglier and funnier than any you have seen.

I used to think I had seen her fanciest and funniest, and her silliest and ugliest gloves.

I used to think I had seen all her most colorful gloves, too. But now I never think that.

As soon as I think that I have seen her fanciest and funniest gloves, she will find fancier.

Being quick may help you be prompt, but it is not the same thing as being prompt.

Being prompt is being ready on time.

Getting ready quickly is not the same thing as getting ready on time.

If you begin to get ready too late, you will be ready late, no matter how quick you are.

Some quick people are often late, if they are not as quick as they think.

When you carry hot food to or from a stove or oven it is often safer to cover the food first.

My brother and I got to ride ponies to go pick berries with Uncle Clover.

Some babies get names in funny ways.

Uncle Clover got his name when the family car broke on the way to the hospital.

Uncle Clover was born on a long lawn of green grass and clover near a lake.

Now that Uncle Clover is big and a dad, he likes to take care of babies.

He likes to pretend he can hear what a baby is thinking and trying to say.

He pretends to go into a trance to say what the baby is trying to say to us as the baby cries.

Aunt Ruby says having a silly name made Uncle Clover like being so silly.

On foggy days I can get lazy. If it is even foggier I like to be even lazier.

On the foggiest days, when the fog is walking on the sidewalks in thick, gray puffs,

I am too lazy to even walk on the sidewalks.

The foggiest days are my laziest days, I sit at a window and write, or read, or do nothing.

That is why I like sunny days. On sunny days I never feel lazy. I like to run and work.

On sunny days, I like running and working and visiting, I am merrier and funnier.

The sunniest days are the days when I am the happiest, not the laziest.

I rode a ferry across the Hudson River. A ferry carries many cars across a wide waterway.

A ferry must be huge to carry lots of cars. It is heavy, even heavier when it is full of cars.

When a ferry is heaviest, when it is carrying the most it can carry, it must be very careful.

When a boat is very heavy, it can only change speed a little bit at a time.

A boat does not use brakes the way a car or bike does. It cannot slow or stop quickly.

The heavier the boat, the slower it is to slow down, and the slower it is to go faster.

A heavy boat can go fast, but it takes it a long time to get going fast.

The heaviest boat can slow down, but it needs the most time and distance to slow down.

You can walk all over the huge ferry and watch the river as the ferry crosses the river.

Then we drove right off the ferry and drove onto the city streets. It is fun to ride a ferry!

When a dog buries its bones, the bones the dog buries in the dirt get dirty.

When my dog brings its dirtiest bones inside after digging them up, the floor gets messy.

So now my dog knows it can only bring its dirty bones inside if it brings the bone secretly.

My dog knows it can't let anyone see its secret dirty bone as it brings the bone inside.

It is hard for a dog to hide a bone it is carrying. Can the dog hide it in a pocket?

I suppose that is why dogs bury bones to hide the bone.

Anyway, now my dog tries to come inside with its dirty bone when we will not see it.

It waits just outside the door listening for us to leave the room, then it brings its bone in.

Can you pick some words from Silent E Team families on this page, then spell their families?

Can you spell the missing adjective endings in the Adjective Family Stories below?

For each blank, say which other words told you whether to spell the ER or the EST ending.

On foggy days I can get lazy. If it is even fogg_____ I like to be even laz_____.

On the fogg_____ days, when the fog is walking on the sidewalks in thick, gray puffs,

I am too lazy to even walk on the sidewalks.

The fogg_____ days are my laz_____ days, I sit at a window and write or read.

On sunny days, I like running and working and visiting, I am merr_____ and funn_____.

The sunn_____ days are the days when I am the happ_____, not the laz_____.

A heavy boat can go fast, but it takes it a long time to get going fast.

A heav____ boat is slow____ to slow down, and slow____ to speed up.

The heav_____ boat can slow down, but uses the most time and distance to do so.

Just when you think you have seen all her gloves, she opens a box full of other gloves.

The other gloves are sill_____, ugl_____, funn_____ and fanc____ than the old gloves.

But just when you think you have seen all her gloves, she opens another box full of gloves.

The next box full is sill_____, fanc_____, funn_____ and ugl____ than any you have seen.

I used to think I had seen her fanc_____, funn_____, sill_____ and ugl_____ gloves.

I used to think I had seen all her most colorful gloves, too. But now I never think that.

As soon as I think I've seen her fanc_____, funn_____ gloves, she'll find fanc_____.

Use pages 127-128 to check your choices above.

Can you fill in the missing adjectives in the families below?

_____	_____	tidy	_____	_____
hazier	_____	_____	_____	hungrier
_____	furriest	_____	wormiest	_____

Can you work as a team to make up an adjective family story for any of those adjective families?

Take turns adding to it. Use page 186 to check your spelling of the 5 adjective families.

There is another ending that works the same way a Silent E ending works. It is a team, not a letter.

It only works if 1 vowel is prior to 1 consonant that is prior to the ending.

This team helps the prior vowel spell that vowel's Name Sound.

It is not silent, like E is.   It spells its usual sound, like Y does.

Read the families on the next two pages with your Reader to figure out what team it is.

Can you draw a line between the words with Name Sounds and the words with Short Sounds?

giggle	wiggle	wriggle	snuggle	tangle	tingle	bugle
giggles	wiggles	wriggles	snuggles	tangles	tingles	bugles
giggling	wiggling	wriggling	snuggling	tangling	tingling	bugling
giggled	wiggled	wriggled	snuggled	tangled	tingled	bugled

tickle	tackle	cackle	buckle	wrinkle	mingle	idle
tickles	tackles	cackles	buckles	wrinkles	mingles	idles
tickling	tackling	cackling	buckling	wrinkling	mingling	idling
tickled	tackled	cackled	buckled	wrinkled	mingled	idled

riddle	struggle	cuddle	belittle	fiddle	enable	cradle
riddles	struggles	cuddles	belittles	fiddles	enables	cradles
riddling	struggling	cuddling	belittling	fiddling	enabling	cradling
riddled	struggled	cuddled	belittled	fiddled	enabled	cradled

handle	bobble	bubble	nibble	scribble	saddle	ladle
handles	bobbles	bubbles	nibbles	scribbles	saddles	ladles
handling	bobbling	bubbling	nibbling	scribbling	saddling	ladling
handled	bobbled	bubbled	nibbled	scribbled	saddled	ladled

All the word families on this page are adjective, noun or verb families. Which? _____

Are any root verbs on this page also roots for noun families? Which ones?

When reading the LE team, which do you say first: the schwa sound E spells or the L sound?

idle	able	little	gentle	ample	supple	simple
idler	abler	littler	gentler	ampler	suppler	simpler
idlest	ablest	littlest	gentlest	amplest	supplest	simplest

staple	cable	babble	rattle	settle	bottle	paddle
staples	cables	babbles	rattles	settles	bottles	paddles
stapling	cabling	babbling	rattling	settling	bottling	paddling
stapled	cabled	babbled	rattled	settled	bottled	paddled

bugle	staple	cradle	fable	puddle	bottle	example
bugles	staples	cradles	fables	puddles	bottles	examples

trifle	sniffle	raffle	ruffle	baffle	whistle	wrestle
trifles	sniffles	raffles	ruffles	baffles	whistles	wrestles
trifling	sniffling	raffling	ruffling	baffling	whistling	wrestling
trifled	sniffled	raffled	ruffled	baffled	whistled	wrestled

stifle	gobble	sizzle	drizzle	dazzle	fi<u>zz</u>le	nestle
stifles	gobbles	sizzles	drizzles	dazzles	fizzles	nestles
stifling	gobbling	sizzling	drizzling	dazzling	fizzling	nestling
stifled	gobbled	sizzled	drizzled	dazzled	fizzled	nestled

sidle	grumble	scramble	crumble	single	double	triple
sidles	grumbles	scrambles	crumbles	singles	doubles	triples
sidling	grumbling	scrambling	crumbling	singling	doubling	tripling
sidled	grumbled	scrambled	crumbled	singled	doubled	tripled

For each root word on these two pages,   do as we did for the verb "fizzle,"

<u>underline</u> the 1 or 2 consonants between the prior vowel and the final LE team.

You have practiced 3 different endings that all work in 1 kind of team to spell a vowel's Name Sound.

This kind of team has 1 vowel prior to 1 consonant prior to any 1 of 3 endings: E, Y or LE.

These 2 pages help you see which families these 3 teams spell name sounds in & which they do not.

If there is only one consonant between prior vowel and ending, the vowel spells its Name Sound.

If there are 2 or more consonants between prior vowel and ending, the vowel spells its Short Sound.

Add the missing root words for the families below. Can you draw a line between short/name vowels?

_____	_____	_____	_____	_____	_____	_____
simpler	sillier	slimmer	wetter	later	nicer	abler
simplest	silliest	slimmest	wettest	latest	nicest	ablest

_____	_____	_____	_____	_____	_____	_____
funnier	happier	hungrier	lazier	cozier	nosier	icier
funniest	happiest	hungriest	laziest	coziest	nosiest	iciest

_____	_____	_____	_____	_____	_____	_____
grins	grabs	runs	swims	times	rhymes	types
grinning	grabbing	running	swimming	timing	rhyming	typing
grinned	grabbed	ran	swam	timed	rhymed	typed

_____	_____	_____	_____	_____	_____	_____
wiggles	tickles	struggles	giggles	crackles	trickles	entitles
wiggling	tickling	struggling	giggling	crackling	trickling	entitling
wiggled	tickled	struggled	giggled	crackled	trickled	entitled

_____	_____	_____	_____	_____	_____	_____
smellier	sunnier	foggier	hazier	scalier	lonelier	pokier
smelliest	sunniest	foggiest	haziest	scaliest	loneliest	pokiest

Can you spell the last two words in each Adjective Family and each Verb Family on this page?

simple	silly	slim	wet	late	nice	able
_____	_____	_____	_____	_____	_____	_____
_____	_____	_____	_____	_____	_____	_____

funny	happy	hungrier	lazy	cozy	nosy	icy
_____	_____	_____	_____	_____	_____	_____
_____	_____	_____	_____	_____	_____	_____

grin	grab	run	swim	time	rhyme	type
grins	grabs	runs	swims	times	rhymes	types
_____	_____	_____	_____	_____	_____	_____
_____	_____	_____	_____	_____	_____	_____

wiggle	tickle	struggle	giggle	crackle	trickle	entitle
wiggles	tickles	struggles	giggles	crackles	trickles	entitles
_____	_____	_____	_____	_____	_____	_____
_____	_____	_____	_____	_____	_____	_____

smelly	sunny	foggy	hazy	scaly	lonely	poky
_____	_____	_____	_____	_____	_____	_____
_____	_____	_____	_____	_____	_____	_____

Use this page to check your spelling on the prior page.

Use the prior page to check your spelling on this page.

Use an adjective from this page in a noun phrase.

Add a verb to your phrase that makes sense with that phrase.

The next two pages show all the different plans you have met so far for spelling verb families.

strum	hum	drum	drag	plug	hug	tug	peg
strum<u>s</u>	hums	drums	drags	plugs	hugs	tugs	peg<u>s</u>
strum<u>ming</u>	humming	drumming	dragging	plugging	hugging	tugging	peg<u>ging</u>
strum<u>med</u>	hummed	drummed	dragged	plugged	hugged	tugged	peg<u>ged</u>

Why do the root words above have short vowel sounds?   (They have no E, Y or LE ending.)

Do we do something extra for any endings above, or do we just add each ending to the root word?

nudge	judge	budge	lodge	edge	pledge	bridge
nudge<u>s</u>	judges	budges	lodges	edges	pledges	bridge<u>s</u>
nudg<u>ing</u>	judging	budging	lodging	edging	pledging	bridg<u>ing</u>
nudg<u>ed</u>	judged	budged	lodged	edged	pledged	bridg<u>ed</u>

Why do the root words above have short vowel sounds?

(They have 2 consonants between the Silent E ending and the prior vowel.)

Do we do something extra for any endings above, or do we just add each ending to the root word?

ask	rest	lick	hand	jump	toss	fizz
asks<u>s</u>	rests	licks	hands	jumps	tosses	fizz<u>es</u>
ask<u>ing</u>	resting	licking	handing	jumping	tossing	fizz<u>ing</u>
ask<u>ed</u>	rested	licked	handed	jumped	tossed	fizz<u>ed</u>

Why do the root words above have short vowel sounds?   (They have no E, Y or LE ending.)

Do we do something extra for any endings above, or do we just add each ending to the root word?

Notice the differences between the top and bottom rows of families.

How many consonants end each root verb in the top row? How many in the bottom row?

What happens with the ING and ED endings in the top row? In the bottom row?

rise	graze	race	close	trace	write	type
rises	grazes	races	closes	traces	writes	types
rising	grazing	racing	closing	tracing	writing	typing
rose	grazed	raced	closed	traced	wrote	typed

Why do the root words above all have a vowel's name sound?

(They have 1 vowel before 1 consonant before a Silent E ending.)

Do we do something extra for any endings above, or do we just add each ending to the root word?

ferry	carry	marry	rely	deny	defy
ferries	carries	marries	relies	denies	defies
ferrying	carrying	marrying	relying	denying	defying
ferried	carried	married	relied	denied	defied

How do we know which of the root words above have short sounds and which have name sounds?

How do we know which of the root words below have short sounds and which have name sounds?

staple	cable	bugle	handle	crumble	paddle
staples	cables	bugles	handles	crumbles	paddles
stapling	cabling	bugling	handling	crumbling	paddling
stapled	cabled	bugled	handled	crumbled	paddled

Can you spell the missing root words in the families below?

The page number below each family tells you where to look to check your spelling of root words.

_____	_____	_____	_____	_____	_____	_____
wrinkles	ladles	tinier	drippier	stops	jokes	jumps
wrinkling	ladling	tiniest	drippiest	stopping	joking	jumping
wrinkled	ladles			stopped	joked	jumped
(Pg. 130)	(Pg. 130)	(Pg. 126)	(Pg. 126)	(Pg. 119)	(Pg. 119)	(Pg. 119)

On these two pages are all the different plans you have met so far for spelling adjective families.

sad	glad	mad	big	thin	red	bad
sadder	gladder	madder	bigger	thinner	redder	worse
saddest	gladdest	maddest	biggest	thinnest	reddest	worst

Why do the root words above have short vowel sounds?   (They have no E, Y or LE ending.)

Do we do something extra for any endings above, or do we just add each ending to the root word?

tense	dense	fancy	jumpy	lumpy	sandy
tenser	denser	fancier	jumpier	lumpier	sandier
tensest	densest	fanciest	jumpiest	lumpiest	sandiest

Why do the root words above have short vowel sounds?

   (They have 2 consonants between the Silent E ending, or the Y ending, and the prior vowel.)

Which final letter of a root adjective do we drop before adding the ER and EST endings? _____

Which final letter of a root adjective do we change before adding the adjective endings?

                                                           __ changes to __.

fast	soft	quick	grand	strong	sick	long
faster	softer	quicker	grander	stronger	sicker	longer
fastest	softest	quickest	grandest	strongest	sickest	longest

Why do the root words above have short vowel sounds?   (They have no E, Y or LE ending.)

Do we do something extra for any endings above, or do we just add each ending to the root word?

Notice the differences between the top ("sad"...) and bottom ("fast"...) rows of adjective families.

How many consonants end the root word in each of the two rows?

What happens with the ER and EST endings in the top row? In the bottom row?

With adjective, noun and verb families, root endings tell spellers which family spelling plan to use.

ripe	nice	close	tame	pale	late		great
ripe	nicer	closer	tamer	paler	later		greater
ripest	nicest	closest	tamest	palest	latest		greatest

Why do the root words to the left of the gap above all have a vowel's name sound?

(They have 1 vowel before 1 consonant before a Silent E ending.)

Do we do something extra for their endings, or do we just add each ending to the root word?

mossy	funny	happy	fancy	icy	spicy	wavy	spiny
mossier	funnier	happier	fancier	icier	spicier	wavier	spinier
mossiest	funniest	happiest	fanciest	iciest	spiciest	waviest	spinest

How do we know which of the root words above have short sounds and which have name sounds?

able	idle		simple	humble	supple	ample
abler	idler		simpler	humbler	suppler	ampler
ablest	idlest		simplest	humblest	supplest	amplest

How do we know which of the root words above have short sounds and which have name sounds?

Can you spell the missing words in the families below? Use the page numbers to check spelling.

———	———	———	———	———	———	———
cuddles	shovels	spinier	sandier	simpler	drives	has
cuddling	shoveling	spiniest	sandiest	simplest	driving	having
cuddled	shoveled				drove	had
(Pg. 130)	(Pg. 122)	(Pg. 137)	(Pg. 136)	(Pg. 137)	(Pg. 122)	(Pg. 113)

———	———	———	———	———	———	———
icier	nicer	quicker	lazier	cozier	rosier	mossier
iciest	nicest	quickest	laziest	coziest	rosiest	mossiest
(Pg. 137)	(Pg. 137)	(Pg. 121)	(Pg. 126)	(Pg. 126)	(Pg. 126)	(Pg. 137)

We call this   **Sound Clues Code.**

A "code" is a different way to write something. This code groups Root Words by their spelling plan.

Our code for a Root Word begins with the vowel or vowels prior to the last consonant.

In the word "plan," "n" is the last consonant, and "a" is the vowel prior to "n", the last consonant.

In the word "dance," "c" is the last consonant, and "a" is the vowel prior to "c", the last consonant.

Below, we have <u>underlined</u> the letters at the end of each word that tell us the word's spelling plan.

     pl<u>an</u>   spr<u>int</u>   pl<u>ane</u>   d<u>ance</u>   f<u>unny</u>   p<u>ony</u>   f<u>able</u>   r<u>iddle</u>

Here are the same Root Words with our code added.

vc	vcc	vc e	vcc e	vcc y	vc y	vc le	vcc le
pl<u>an</u>	spr<u>int</u>	pl<u>ane</u>	d<u>ance</u>	f<u>unny</u>	p<u>ony</u>	f<u>able</u>	r<u>iddle</u>

What does "v" mean in our code? Any <u>v</u>owel is coded as a "v", unless it is in a family or root ending.

What does "c" mean in our code? Any <u>c</u>onsonant is coded with a "c", unless in a family or root ending.

E, Y or LE are root endings.   S ES ING ED ER EST are family endings.

If a root word ends with an E, Y or LE ending,

                     find the consonant or consonants before the ending,

     and   begin coding with the vowel or vowels just before that.

If the word ends with a consonant, code the prior vowel and all the letters after it.

The letters we code are the same letters we use to know which family spelling plan a family uses.

Can you <u>underline</u> the words below whose first vowel spells its own name sound?

Can you code the 1st Root Word in each pair of words below?

Does the 2nd Root Word in each pair have the same code name that the 1st Root Word in its <u>pair</u> has?

candle	able	cane	fence	penny	tiny	stand	nut
rattle	idle	cone	ledge	happy	baby	rest	drip

You can compare your code to ours by looking at the bottom of the next page.

That is   **Sound Clues Code.**   Use it to compare family spelling plans in any Chapter.

We call this   **Family Finisher.**

Fold a blank paper in half twice vertically and twice horizontally, so the folds separate 16 sections.

On the top line of each of the 16 sections write a root verb from any verb family in any chapter.

Next to the root verb write the page number you found the verb family on.

Study the spelling plan of the family.

Try to decide which spelling plan the family is using as you study each family.

Can you use our Sound Clues Code to code the root verb on your paper after you write it down?

Now add the other 3 verbs for each verb family in all 16 sections.

Use the page numbers you wrote to check your spelling of the 16 verb families after you write them.

Correct any words you misspelled as you check your spelling.

Use this same activity with adjective families as well.

The first dozen times you do this, you may prefer to practice 1 family spelling plan for the whole page.

That is   **Family Finisher.**

Celebrate finishing Chapter 5 by reading any or all of the following books.

I Stink	Kate & Jim McMullan
My Brother, Ant	Betsy Byars
Everett Anderson's 1-2-3	Lucille Clifton, Ann Grifalconi
Babies On the Go	Linda Ashman, Jane Dyer
One Grain of Sand: A Lullaby	Pete Seeger, Linda Wingerter

Below is our coding of the root words you coded at the bottom of the previous page.

vcc le	vc le	vc e	vcc e	vcc y	vc y	vcc	vc
candle	able	cane	fence	penny	tiny	stand	nut
rattle	idle	cone	ledge	happy	baby	rest	drip

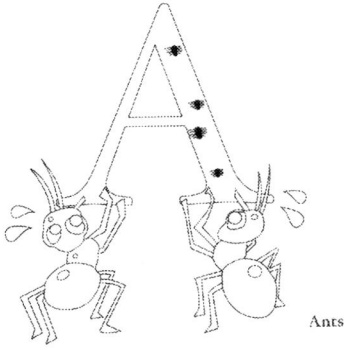

Ants

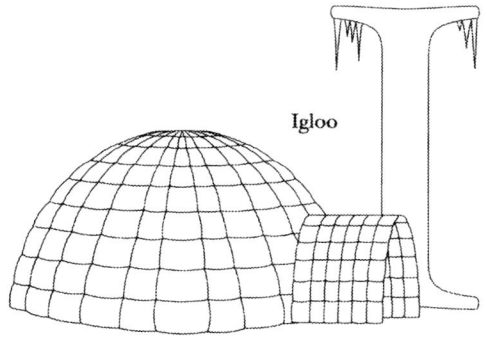

Igloo

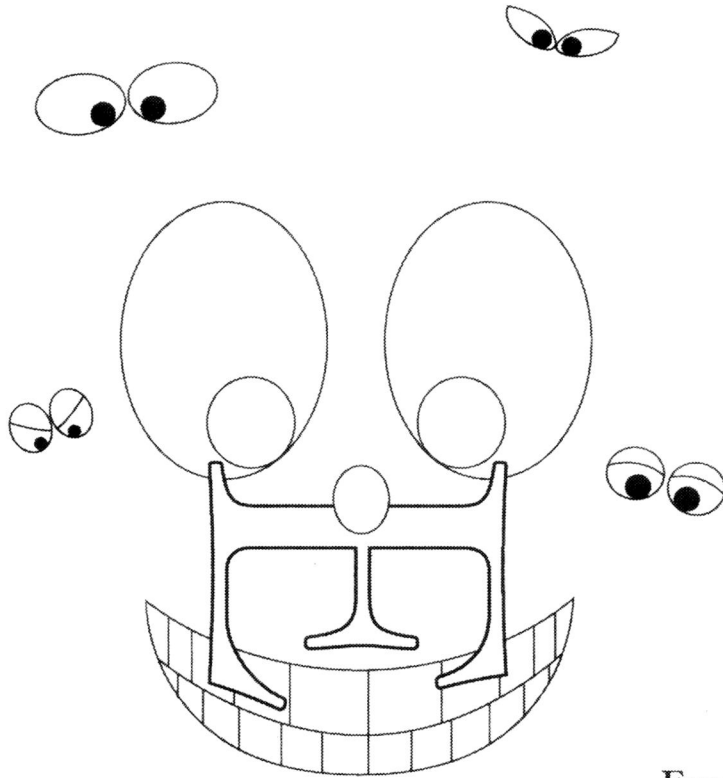

Eyes

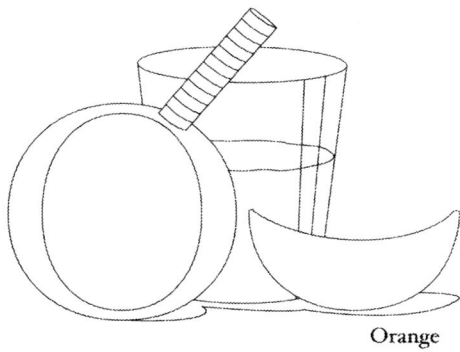

Orange

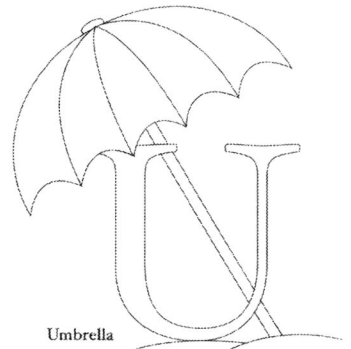

Umbrella

Chapter 6

Our Goals for Chapter 6 are:

- Continue to practice (w) and the team (qu).
        (pp. 146 - 163 , 166)
- Notice "usual" and "unusual" spelling patterns.
        (pp. 144 - 163 , 166)
- **Hear all the "weird ways" A and O sometimes spell different sounds when they follow W.**
        (pp. 148 - 149 , 152 – 163, 166)
- Meet and practice the only 4 words in which a vowel spells a consonant sound.
        (pp. 148 – 151, 162 – 163)
- Briefly hear the "weird ways" that (al ar) spell after (w) and (qu).
        (pp. 156 - 159 , 166)
- Study and practice which member of an Adjective Family to use when.
        (pp. 155 - 156 , 159 - 161)
- Continue studying and practicing which member of a Noun Family to use when.
        (pp. 150 - 151 , 157 , 159 , 161)
- Continue studying and practicing which member of a Verb Family to use when.
        (pp. 149 - 151 , 153 – 161)
- Meet the Five Questions that stories answer.
        (pp. 164 – 165)

Here are some Practice Suggestions you may want to try:

Practicing alphabetical order is good preparation for beginning to use a dictionary.

Words Lists that rhyme can provide excellent spelling practice.

Work together to write lists of words that all rhyme with each other.

Stick to words with only one or two vowel sounds.

After you have made a list as long as you can, work together to re-write your list in alphabetical order.

When re-writing a list, Reader should help by asking questions; let Learner find each next word.

Practice Calendar
Chapter 6

Day & Date	Time	Page	Notes, Comments

A wick is the string in the wax of a candle, the bit that sticks up from the top and burns.

The wax of the candle will not burn with no wick for the wax to cling to.

The wick burns too fast if it has no wax. A wick with no wax is no wick, it is just string.

I wonder if a wick burns better if one twists the wick first.

Will a twisted wick burn better than an untwisted wick?

My dog wags its tail fast when it is happy.

My dog wags its tail faster when it is happier.

My dog wags its tail fastest when it is happiest.

My frog will not wag its tail at all when it is happier than my dog.

My frog will not wag its tail at all even if it is the happiest pet in our city.

My frog will not wag its tail when it is happy.   Why not?

Do frogs have tails they can wag?

Willy's dog is bigger and faster than Jerry's dog.

Jerry's dog is bigger than Wanda's dog, but not as fast.

Willy's dog is bigger than Jerry's dog and Wanda's dog.

Willy's dog is faster than Jerry's dog, but not as fast as Wanda's dog.

Whose dog is fastest: Jerry's, Willy's or Wanda's?

My frog Vicky hops longer and faster hops than my frog Vince.

My frog Velma sings longer every day than my frogs Vance, Vicky and Vince.

Vicky and Vince are Velma's and Vance's mom and dad. Do you ever listen to frogs sing?

Vance runs faster than Vance's father. Vance's mother runs faster than Vance.

Who runs faster, Vance's father or Vance's mother?

(Is the Vance in this story the same Vance that was in the last story?)

Wally sings better than Wilma. Wilma sings better than Walter.

Does Wally sing better than Wilma or Walter?

Can you get any ideas from this page for writing your own Adjective Family Stories?

An important pair of words to understand, when talking about spelling, are "**Usual**" and "**Unusual**." Study these underlined examples of letters spelling in "**usual**" and "**unusual**" ways.

Usual						**Unusual**		
<u>f</u>ox	<u>f</u>inger	a<u>f</u>ter	so<u>f</u>t	ski<u>ff</u>		o<u>f</u>		

abo<u>v</u>e	glo<u>v</u>e	co<u>v</u>er	do<u>v</u>e		o<u>f</u>	

adds	fills	misses	purrs	stubs		fits	stuffs
hug<u>s</u>	slam<u>s</u>	open<u>s</u>	nudge<u>s</u>		camp<u>s</u>	pack<u>s</u>

sing	give	ride	save	sell	wave		have
sing<u>s</u>	give<u>s</u>	ride<u>s</u>	save<u>s</u>	sell<u>s</u>	wave<u>s</u>		<u>has</u>
singing	giving	riding	saving	selling	waving		having
sang	gave	rode	saved	sold	waved		had

span	fan	pin	stun		spin	run	begin
spans	fans	pins	stuns		spins	runs	begins
spanning	fanning	pinning	stunning		spinning	running	beginning
span<u>ned</u>	fan<u>ned</u>	pin<u>ned</u>	stun<u>ned</u>		sp<u>u</u>n	r<u>a</u>n	beg<u>a</u>n

cat	dog	rabbit	fox	kid	squirrel		squid	child	person
cats	dogs	rabbits	foxes	kids	squirrels		squid	children	people

"Usual" means "most often" or "almost always." "Unusual" means "sometimes, but not often."

S spelling the Z sound at the end of "gives" is usual.

I's short sound in "gives" is unusual. Why would I spelling I's name sound in "gives" be usual?

Each statement below describes a pair of "usual" and "unusual" spelling patterns from page 144. Can you use the numbers to match each statement below with a row of examples from page 144?

(1)   Plural nouns usually end with S. It is unusual when a plural noun does not end with an S.

(2)   We usually spell an S-ending verb by just adding S or ES to the end of the root verb.

        This is the only S-ending verb whose spelling is not "by the plan."

(3)   This consonant almost always spells its own sound, except in one unusual word.

(4)   This consonant sound is almost always spelled by its consonant, except in **1** unusual word.

(5)   A consonant that adds meaning to root words, usually spells another consonant's sound. It is unusual for this consonant to spell its own sound when added to a root word.

(6)   When a verb family is not spelled "by the plan," the unusual verb is usually the Past Verb.

Were you able to match each statement above with a row of examples from page 144?

What is unusual about the verb families to the right below, when compared to the families to the left?

Usual						Unusual	
ripple	fiddle	topple	grapple	idle	staple	triple	
ripples	fiddles	topples	grapples	idles	staples	triples	
rippling	fiddling	toppling	grappling	idling	stapling	tripling	
rippled	fiddled	toppled	grappled	idled	stapled	tripled	
time	stripe	bite	like	write	ride	pass	type	rhyme
times	stripes	bite	likes	writes	rides	passes	types	rhymes
timing	striping	biting	liking	writing	riding	passing	typing	rhyming
timed	striped	bite	liked	wrote	rode	passed	typed	rhymed

Wall

Remember me?   My name is W.

My W sound is easy to read.

But the words I am in are not easy to read.

Unless you recognize them.   Why is that?

Vowels do not spell normally around me!

I will tell you a little about the ways that vowels spell next to me.

You will see it is not the same ways they spell around other letters.

When my Letter friends want to tease me, they have a saying they say.

They say, "W spells Weird Words!"

I don't mind. I just tell them they are jealous of what a special speller I am.

Do not worry about remembering exactly what I tell you in the next several pages.

There are a lot of weird ways the vowels spell different sounds after me than they usually spell.

But there are very few words that are spelled each of those weird ways!

It is not worth the trouble to remember all those rules that only work for a few words.

The examples on the next pages are most of the words those rules work in!

You'll learn to recognize & remember my weird words without rules, by reading the words in sentences.

Just like you learn to spell some words just by reading them often.

You learned to read my W sound by reading "we," "was," "went," "will," and "were."

Just remember. W spells "Weird Words."

Practice them and you will know them when you see them, and spell them as soon as you think them.

Here is one weird part about being W.

For reasons hundreds of years old,

      that we have both forgotten,

      U is never next to me when we spell words.

U is never after me in English words. U is never before me.

I is another vowel that is never before me.

I didn't do anything to them! Really! They are not mad at me!

We just never work next to each other spelling in English words.

I don't know why! English became English hundreds of years ago.

People made English, by talking with each other, from words of other languages those people spoke.

Letters did not invent English. We are only tools you can write it with, if you can spell us.

So, I is never before me when I spell in words, but I can follow me in words.

I spells very normally when I follows me in words.

wit	wig	will	twist	win	wick	swim
winter	wiggle	wind	twig	twins	wing	swift

The twins can swim swiftly, but not in a river in the winter.

                    Birds have the wit to twist twigs together in a nest.

The wick on a candle will burn.

                    Wax on the candle wick helps a wick burn longer.

A wick wet with wax will burn even in the wind, until the wind gets fast and strong.

                    The winter winds whistled as they bent and twisted the twigs.

Winter wind will wiggle twigs and can whistle a little, but it will not swim.

                    When will swift swimming win?

W here again.

Sometimes A and O spell U's short sound after me.

was   wasn't   won

wonder   wonders   wondering   wondered

Wall

In the next row of words, O spells my W sound **and** U's short sound!

one   ones   one's   once

Those are the only words where a vowel spells a consonant sound!

Since we just learned the number "one," this is a good time for another "weird" word with "wo" in it.

two

Two other words sound exactly like the number.   too   to

We will practice reading all three words, and the other words above, for the next few pages.

When you practice, remember, the number "two" is the Weird Word with me, W, in it.

Which of the words below with W are not weird?

Which of the words below with W are weird?

wonder   win   swim   twist

wonders   wins   swims   twists

wondering   winning   swimming   twisting   was

wondered   won   swam   twisted

went   when   whenever   what   whatever

Choose one of the 4 words on the right to fill each of the blanks below.   wonder

wonders

wondering

I wonder if I can jump off that log.   wondered

Jack _____ if he can jump off of two logs.

Jerry and Janet _____ if they can jump off the small hill of dirt by our front steps.

We are wondering if anyone jumps off of that small dirt hill by our steps.

Will is _____ if he can jump longer jumps than his dog.

Timmy is _____ if he can jump longer jumps than Will's dog.

Yesterday I wondered if I had two cents or one cent.

Yesterday Sally _____ if she had one cent, two cents or ten cents.

I am wondering if Wilma is winning. We are all wondering if Wilma is winning.

After the run was over, I was wondering if Wilma won. We were all wondering.

We wondered if Wilma won until we saw Walt was the winner. We stopped wondering.

The first winner, Walt, won once, then a different winner won the second run.

The first two winners did not win the third run. Another winner won the third run.

The second winner won the fourth run. It was the second time she won.

The first and third winners won once, but did not win any other runs.

"Once you have won one run, you will want to win once more," said the first winner.

"Once you have won two runs, you still want to win once more," said the second winner.

Then the third winner said, "If you win a third run, you will still want to win once more."

One winner won two runs, and two winners won once. All the winners ran four runs.

Will winning once stop one from wanting to win?

Did winning two runs stop the second winner from wanting to win once more?

Once you win one race, will you stop wanting to win in the races you run?

Once you win two races, will you stop wanting to win any races you run?

Once you have won three races you ran, will you stop wanting to run in and win races?

One whistle whistles. Two whistles whistle. Six whistles whistle. Ten whistles whistle.

One whistler's whistle whistles. Two whistlers' whistles whistle.

One wiggly twin wiggles. Two wiggly twins wiggle. Yesterday the wiggly twins wiggled.

Once one dancer dances, the next dancer dances.

Once one dancer dances, the other two dancers dance.

Once one singer sings, the other two singers sing.

Once one singer sings, the other one sings.

Once one singer sings, the other ones sing.

Once one jumper jumps rope, the other jumpers jump rope.

Once one jogger jogs, two other joggers jog.

Once one jogger jogs, the other ones jog.

Once one jogger jogs, the other one jogs.

Once one twin wins, the other twin wants to win.

Once one twin swims, the other twin wants to swim.

"Seven times one" tells you to add seven ones together.

"Ten times one" tells you to add ten ones together.

"Six times one" tells you to add six ones together.

"Eleven times one" tells you to add eleven ones together.

"Twelve times one" tells you to add twelve ones together.

"Twelve times two" tells you to add twelve twos together.

"Seven times two" tells you to add seven twos together.

"Six times two" tells you to add six twos together.

"Two times six" tells you to add two sixes together. Six plus six is twelve.

"Two times ten" tells you to add two tens together. Ten plus ten is twenty.

"Two times two" tells you to add two twos together. Two plus two is four.

"Two times seven" tells you to add two sevens together. Seven plus seven is fourteen.

"Three times five" tells you to add three fives together. Three times five is fifteen.

Decide, for each blank, if it needs an "s" in it for the sentence to make sense. If it does, write the "s".

One whistle whistles. Two whistles whistle. Six whistles whistle. Ten whistle__ whistle__ .

One whistler's whistle whistles. Two whistlers' whistle__ whistle__ .

One wiggly twin wiggle__ . Two wiggly twins wiggle__ .

Once one dancer__ dance__, the next dancer dance__ .

Once one dancer__ dance__, the other two dancers dance__ .

Once one singer__ sing__, the other two singers sing__ .

Once one singer__ sing__, the other one sing__ .

Once one singer__ sing__, the other ones sing__ .

Once one jumper__ jump__ rope, the other jumpers jump__ rope.

Once one jogger__ jog__, two other joggers jog__ .

Once one jogger__ jog__, the other ones jog__ .

Once one jogger__ jog__, the other one jog__ .

Once one twin__ win__, the other twin want__ to win.

Once one twin__ swim__, the other twin want__ to swim.

One plus one is two times one. Six plus six is two time__ six.

One plus one plus one plus one plus one plus one is six time__ one.

Two plus two plus two plus two plus two plus two is six time__ two.

Six plus six plus six plus six plus six plus six is six time__ six.

Six plus six plus six plus six plus six plus six plus six is seven times six__ .

Seven plus seven plus seven plus seven plus seven plus seven is six time__ seven.

Two plus two plus two plus two plus two plus two plus two is seven__ times two__ .

One plus one plus one plus one plus one plus one plus one is seven time__ one.

Seven plus seven is two__ time__ seven__ . Ten plus ten is two__ time__ ten__ .

W here still, with more of my weird words.

There are not very many words that begin with WA.

Sometimes A spells O's short sound after me.

Wall

wan	want	wander	wad	waddle
	wants	wanders	wads	waddles
waffle	wanting	wandering	wadding	waddling
waffles	wanted	wandered	wadded	waddled

A spells A's short sound after me in some words.   A spells U's short sound in some words.

wag	wax	waggle	what	was
wags	waxes	waggles	whatever	wasn't
wagging	waxing	waggling	somewhat	
wagged	waxed	waggled		

When A follows W you have to think of all the sounds A might be spelling.

Then you think, "Which of the sounds that A might be spelling helps the other letters spell a word."

Next, you have to think, "Does that word make sense in the sentence?"

If the word you thought of doesn't make sense in the sentence, what other sound could A be spelling?

It will not be as hard to figure out which sound A is spelling in a word as it was to read about it here.

The more often you read words, the more easily & quickly you'll remember them when you see them.

How many different sounds does A spell as it follows me, W, in the Words Lists above?   ____

Choose one of the 4 words on the right to fill each of the blanks below.   wander

wanders

wandering

I wander whenever I get to go to the city.   wandered

I _____ in the city last Saturday.

I will _____ in the city next Saturday too.

I was wandering in the city two Saturdays ago when I met Warren and Walter.

Warren _____ in the city every Saturday. Walter _____ then too.

Some Saturdays Walter, Warren and Wilma _____ in the city together.

Some Saturdays Walter, Warren and Wilma do not _____ together.

Next Saturday Wilma will be _____ in the city with Warren, but not Walter.

Whenever I wander in the hills I wonder what animals live in the hills.

When my sister wanders in the hills she wonders what insects live in the hills.

When my brother wanders in the hills he wonders what birds live in the hills.

When my mother wanders in the hills she wonders what plants live in the hills.

Whenever the others in my family wander in the hills, they wonder what lives in the hills.

We also wonder what was living in the hills fifty or seventy or a hundred years ago.

Do the critters that wander in these hills wonder who wandered here sixty years ago?

I wanted to warn my brother not to wander away from where Mom and Dad were.

I warned my brother not to wander, and was there with him when he warned my sister.

My sister wondered why we were warning her not to wander, when she never wandered.

As our sister wondered, my brother and I wandered off to warn other kids not to wander.

As we wandered the vicinity warning all the other kids not to wander, Mom left to go visit.

Dad waited at home for us to be done wandering the vicinity warning kids not to wander.

We told Dad what we'd done. He told us two kids didn't get our warning not to wander.

We wondered how he knew. We wondered which two kids we hadn't warned not to wander.

Who were the two kids who missed our warning not to wander?

You can compare the verb choices you made on page 149 with our choices here.

wonder

wonders

wondering

I wonder if I can jump off that log.   wondered

Jack __wonders__ if he can jump off of two logs.

Jerry and Janet __wonder__ if they can jump off the small hill of dirt by our front steps.

We are wondering if anyone jumps off of that small dirt hill by our steps.

Will is __wondering__ if he can jump longer jumps than his dog.

Timmy is __wondering__ if he can jump longer jumps than Will's dog.

Yesterday I wondered if I had two cents or one cent.

Yesterday Sally __wondered__ if she had one cent, two cents or ten cents.

You can compare the verb choices you made on page 153 with our choices here.

wander

wanders

wandering

I wander whenever I get to go to the city.   wandered

I __wandered__ in the city last Saturday.

I will __wander__ in the city next Saturday too.

I was wandering in the city two Saturdays ago when I met Warren and Walter.

Warren __wanders__ in the city every Saturday. Walter __wanders__ then too.

Some Saturdays Walter, Warren and Wilma __wander__ in the city together.

Some Saturdays Walter, Warren and Wilma do not __wander__ together.

Next Saturday Wilma will be __wandering__ in the city with Warren, but not Walter.

Can you continue either of these stories by adding to them in your Notebook?

I love waffles. Waffles are the yummiest snack I love.

And waffles get yummier with melted butter on top.

Waffles are yummier with melted butter and blackberry jam than just with melted butter.

My waffles are yummiest with bananas and apples in the waffle batter.

My sister runs faster than I do. I run faster than my brother runs.

Who runs faster, my sister or my brother?

Yesterday I watered my plants. Yesterday my sister watered her plants.

My sister and I were watering our plants yesterday, just before dinner.

Yesterday my Mom watered her plants. Yesterday my Dad watered his plants.

My Mom and Dad were watering their plants after dinner yesterday, and today too.

They will try to water their big plants and their small plants on Saturday and Sunday.

My sister waters my plants when I go away from home. I water her plants when she goes.

My son gets water from my well to mix into our waffle batter. We will have waffles today.

"I am so hungry I can swallow all of my waffles in one swallow," I said to my dad.

My dad said, "If you swallow all of your waffles in one swallow, it is all you will get."

I did not swallow all of my waffles in one swallow. I wanted to get "seconds" of waffles.

I have had my "seconds" of waffles, but I think today I have to have "thirds" of waffles.

My sister and I like to jump. We like to jump up. We like to jump down.

We try to jump up onto small walls without using our hands.

We can jump onto walls that are two feet tall. If we fall off we do not get hurt.

Walls that are three feet tall are too tall to jump up onto, even using our hands.

The jumping we like best is to jump off of small walls, walls that are one or two feet tall.

We like jumping off of small walls onto soft dirt and deep green grass, but not falling off.

But the best jumping of all the jumping we do is when we jump rope.

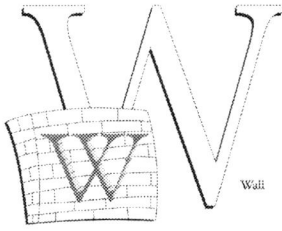

Hi. **W** here. And still talking about weird ways **A** spells when **A** follows me.

In words that start with **WAL**, **A** spells the sound **A** spells in the **ALL** team.

ball	call	tall	fall	wall	Walt	Walter
balls	calls	taller	falls	walls	Walt's	Walter's
	calling	tallest	falling			
	called		fell			

When a word starts **WAR**, the **AR** team spells the **OR** team's sound, the word "or."

You will meet and practice the **AR** and **OR** teams' sounds in Volume 3.

Practice these "weird words" that begin with **WAR**. Do you hear the **AR** team spell the word "or"?

The **AR** team only spells that sound when it follows **W** !

warm	warm	warn	warp	warmth	wart	war
warmer	warms	warns	warps		warts	wars
warmest	warming	warning	warping			
	warmed	warned	warped			

Choose one of the 7 words on the right to fill each of the blanks below.

warm	warm
warms	warmer
warming	warmest
warmed	

I love _____ waffles.

I will _____ waffles and cut apples and bananas for our waffles next Sunday.

Jack _____ our waffles every Saturday.

Jerry and Janet _____ our waffles last Monday and last Thursday.

The _____ waffles melt the butter the fastest.

The waffles I _____ yesterday were _____ than our waffles are today.

When a QU team is before AR, QU sounds like KW, and AR sounds just like it does after W.

quart		quarter	quarter	quarrel	quarrel
quarts		quarters	quarters	quarrels	quarrels
			quartering		quarreling
			quartered		quarreled

Here are some sentences to practice reading some of the words above.

I said I was faster than my sister.

My sister said she was faster than me.

Once both of us said we were the fastest one, we began to quarrel.

As we quarreled we began to yell, "I am the fastest!"

I yelled, "I am the fastest!" at my sister.

My sister yelled, "I am faster than you!" at me.

We quarreled until our mom yelled at us.

"Stop yelling and stop quarreling!" our mom yelled.

"No more quarrels between you two today!" our mom yelled. "And no more yelling!"

"The first one of you to quarrel or yell will have to go to bed until dinner!" yelled Mom.

A quarter is a quarter of a dollar, one-fourth of a dollar. Four quarters is a dollar.

A quart of milk is one quarter of a gallon of milk.

A gallon of milk has four quarts of milk in it.

If you quarter an apple you cut the apple into four pieces.

Every one of the four pieces is one quarter of the apple.

My brother quarters melons at his job by cutting every melon into four pieces.

The melons he has quartered are called "melon quarters."

He is quartering melons at his job as I am telling you that he quarters melons.

She will water her plants after she fills her watering can with water.

She waters her plants every day until her watering can is empty.

I fill my watering can with water every day before I water my plants.

I water my plants every day until my watering can is empty.

We water the plants every day until we have no water in our cans to water them with.

She waters her plants until she empties all the water from her watering can.

I water my plants until I empty all the water from my watering can.

We water our plants until we give all the water in our watering cans to the thirsty plants.

Our brother waters his plants until he empties his watering can twice.

Our mother will water her plants every day until she empties her watering can twice.

My sister has watered her plants every day since she was bigger than her biggest plant.

I said to my mom, "I am hungry!" Then I asked her for a snack.

My mom said, "I will warm a bit of milk, and cut a quarter of an apple for you."

She warmed the milk and cut an apple into four quarters.

Two quarters were for me and two quarters were for her.

She said, "When you cut an apple into four quarters, that is called quartering the apple."

I asked, "If I cut the milk into four quarters, is that called quartering the milk?"

My mom giggled a little bit and said, "You are being silly. Since when can you cut milk?"

I said, "I have to cut the milk with my lips and my teeth every swallow of milk I drink."

My mom had warmed my milk. She handed me a quarter of the apple and the warm milk.

She did not say anything more as she handed me the cup of warm milk and apple quarter.

Are a quarter of an apple and a cup of warm milk better if they come from your mom?

You may want to review what Articles are at the bottom of page 86 before trying this activity.

First, underline every Article on this page, then copy one story with blanks replacing all the Articles.

Photocopy it if you can. Save it for a few days.

After a few days, fill in the blanks. Compare your choices to the story.

Were your Articles the same as we used in our story?

Do your Articles agree with their Noun Phrases?   Which is important? Which is not?

On page 156 you filled the blanks of this verb family & adjective family story of the root word "warm."

Read the story here, then re-read the story on page 156. Change any words you need to change.

I love warm waffles.

I will warm waffles and cut apples and bananas for our waffles next Sunday.

Jack warms our waffles every Saturday.

Jerry and Janet warmed our waffles last Monday and last Thursday.

The warmest waffles melt the butter the fastest.

The waffles I warmed yesterday were warmer than our waffles are today.

Use the verb family and noun family of "quarter" to fill in all the blanks you can in the story below.

Next, re-read the same story on page 157, then fill in any blanks below you could not fill at first.

Use page 157 to check all of your choices of words to fill the blanks below.

A _____ is a _____ of a dollar, one-fourth of a dollar. Four _____ is a dollar.

A quart of milk is one _____ of a gallon of milk.

A gallon of milk has four quarts of milk in it.

If you _____ an apple you cut the apple into four pieces.

Every one of the four pieces is one _____ of the apple.

My brother _____ melons at his job by cutting every melon into four pieces.

The melons he has _____ are called "melon _____."

He is _____ melons at his job while I am telling you that he _____ melons.

Repeat the above practice for the verb family "warm" and the noun and verb families of "quarter."

Use page 158 to correct your work.

My mom said, "I will _____ a bit of milk, and cut a _____ of an apple for you."

She _____ the milk and cut an apple into four _____.

Two _____ were for me and two _____ were for her.

She said cutting an apple into four _____ is called _____ the apple.

I asked, "If I cut the milk into four _____, is that called _____ the milk?"

Fill the blanks as you read a story, re-read the original story, then re-read the story below.

Page 155 has this Verb Family Story of "water."

Yesterday I _____ my plants. Yesterday my sister _____ her plants.

My sister and I were _____ our plants yesterday, just before dinner.

Yesterday my Mom _____ her plants. Yesterday my Dad _____ his plants.

My Mom and Dad were _____ their plants after dinner yesterday, and today too.

They will try to _____ their big plants and their small plants on Saturday and Sunday.

My sister _____ my plants when I go away. I _____ her plants when she is away.

This story from page 153 has two verb families, "wander" or "wonder," that fill the blanks.

Whenever I _____ in the hills I _____ what animals live in the hills.

When my sister _____ in the hills she _____ what insects live in the hills.

When my brother _____ in the hills he _____ what birds live in the hills.

When my mother _____ in the hills she _____ what plants live in the hills.

When others in my family _____ in the hills, they _____ what lives in the hills.

We also _____ what was living in the hills fifty or seventy or a hundred years ago.

Do the critters that _____ in these hills _____ who _____ here sixty years ago?

This story from page 143 needs its blanks filled with the adjective families "happy" and "fast."

My dog wags its tail _____ when it is _____.

My dog wags its tail _____ when it is _____.

My dog wags its tail _____ when it is _____.

My frog will not wag its tail at all when it is _____ than my dog.

My frog will not wag its tail at all, even if it is the _____ pet in our city.

My frog will not wag its tail when it is _____.   Why not?

Do frogs have tails they can wag?

Fill the blanks as you read a story, re-read the original story, the re-read the story below.

The adjective family "fast" and the verb family "yell" have been blanked in this story from page 157.

I said I was _____ than my sister.

My sister said she was _____ than me.

Once both of us said we were the _____ one, we began to quarrel.

As we quarreled we began to _____, "I am the _____!"

I _____, "I am the _____!" at my sister.

My sister _____, "I am _____ than you!" at me.

We quarreled until our mom _____ at us.

"Stop _____ and stop quarreling!" our mom _____.

"No more quarrels between you two today!" our mom _____. "And no more _____!"

The noun and verb families for the root word "water" have been blanked in this story from page 158.

She will _____ her plants after she fills her watering can with _____.

She _____ her plants every day until her watering can is empty.

I fill my watering can with _____ every day before I _____ my plants.

I _____ my plants every day until my watering can is empty.

We always _____ the plants until we have no _____ left to _____ them with.

She _____ her plants until she empties all the _____ from her watering can.

I _____ my plants until I empty all the _____ from my watering can.

We _____ our plants until all the _____ in our watering cans is under the plants.

Our brother _____ his plants until he empties his watering can twice.

Our mother will _____ her plants every day until she empties her watering can twice.

My sister has _____ her plants every day since she was bigger than her biggest plant.

Was it easy for you to fill in the blanks with the correct verb or noun?

When you checked your work, did you have to change some of your word choices?

If you do these same pages again, will it be easier to choose correctly, or will it be harder?

Here is a page that will let you practice the sounds vowels make near W in "W's Weird Words."

wag	Wes	wall	well	wig
wags	wet	walls	welt	wit
wax	wed	Walt	weld	wilt
waxes	wets	Walt's	welds	will
waxing	weds	Walter	welts	willing

was	won	wonder	wonders	wondering	wondered

what	one	ones	once	one's

wan	want	wad	waddle	waffle
	wants	wads	waddles	waffles
	wanting		waddling	
	wanted		waddled	

wag	wags	wax	waxes	waxing	waft	wafting
wall	walls	Walt	Walt's	Walter	Walter's	
war	warn	warm	warmer	warmest	warming	warning

wit	wig	will	wilt	win	wick	wing
wiggle	winter	wind	twig	swig	swim	swift

How many of these words can you use in sentences?

Look up some of the words in a dictionary for fun.

Can you say the whole family for the words in the Words Lists at the top and bottom?

Can you colorize the vowel sounds on this page?

Use page 187 to choose your tools. Use page 194 to check your choices.

wag	Wes	wall	well	wig
wags	wet	walls	welt	wit
wax	wed	Walt	weld	wilt
waxes	wets	Walt's	welds	will
waxing	weds	Walter	welts	willing

was	won	wonder	wonders	wondering	wondered

what	one	ones	once	one's

wan	want	wad	waddle	waffle
	wants	wads	waddles	waffles
	wanting		waddling	
	wanted		waddled	

wag	wags	wax	waxes	waxing	waft	wafting
wall	walls	Walt	Walt's	Walter	Walter's	
war	warn	warm	warmer	warmest	warming	warning

wit	wig	will	wilt	win	wick	wing
wiggle	winter	wind	twig	swig	swim	swift

Do you see why my Letter friends say, "W stands for Weird Words!"?

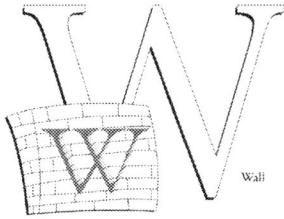

As I've said, " W stands for Weird Words!" Now you know why.

Remember not to worry about remembering all the "rules" we explained.

Very few words spell using the "rules" that make W words weird.

Most of my weird words you will read so often that you will soon remember them easily, automatically.

You will soon learn to recognize them just by reading them. **This happens faster if you read often!**

You probably don't remember the special thing the WH team does.

We mentioned it briefly, on page 98 Of Vol. 1, but didn't practice it, so you may not remember it.

With LE, you say E's schwa sound before you say L's sound, even though L comes first in the team.

With WH, you say the H sound, then W's sound. None of H's other consonant teams do that.

You will meet and practice all of H's many consonant teams in Chapter 11.

Our WH team is very special in another way, but this time I am not special for being in weird words.

Our WH team starts the 5 words that start the 5 purposes of every story and every sentence.

Our five WH questions are so special because they are so important!

Every story should try to answer all 5 of our WH questions.

Every sentence should answer some of them!

Listen carefully as your Reader reads the 5 question-words, which all begin with the WH team.

Say which of the 5 question-words doesn't start with our WH sound.

Who?   What?   When?   Where?   Why?

If you heard the question "Who?" for the first time, you would think it was spelled "Hoo?"

Boo hoo!   Boo who?   Who boos?   Who are you?

Re-read some stories and say which WH questions each story answered.

I'm W ! I begin the most important questions. And a lot of useful but weirdly spelled words, too!

We call this   **WH Q**s.

You may prefer to call it   **5 + 1 WH Q**s.

List 5 **WH** questions down the left edge of a blank paper or Notebook page, with spaces between.

Pick a story you like.

Read the story, listening for the answer to each of the 5 **WH** questions as you read the story.

Tap the table with a finger each time you hear information about one of the 5 **WH** questions.

When you finish the story, write the answer to each question where you listed it.

After answering all the questions you can, set the story and your answers aside for a day or two.

After a day or 2, take out the page where you wrote the 5 questions and those answers the story gave.

Write the 5 questions on another blank paper, in the same order.

You may have answers on the original page to all 5 of the questions, or only some of the 5.

Copy the answers you do have onto your new page, except for one!

Choose one of the answers from the original story to change. Write a new answer to that question.

Then write answers on the new page for any questions the original story did not answer.

Now read all 5 answers from your new page. Do all 5 answers make sense together?

(If "<u>What</u>?" is "swimming," and "<u>Where</u>?" is "the sky," they don't!)

If any 2 of the 5 answers don't make sense together, change one so they do make sense together.

Now that you have answers to all 5 storytelling questions that make sense together, retell the story.

If you decide you really like the story the way you retold it, write the story down in your Notebook.

Ask your Reader or teacher to check your spelling, **<u>after</u>** you try to spell all the words yourself.

That is   **WH Q**s,

or, if you prefer,   **5 + 1 WH Q**s.

We call this   **Dictionary Research.**

Not many words begin with WA or WO, and those words are all together in the dictionary.

Try to find a children's dictionary that includes examples of sentences that use the words.

Compare several different children's dictionaries at the local public library.

Find the WA words and read all the meanings and sample sentences for words that start with WA.

Now find the WO words & read all the meanings & sample sentences for words that start with WO.

Reading all the WA and WO words' definitions and sample sentences will help you remember them.

Make up your own sentences with examples of how to use the words in each family you look up.

Do a different section of the dictionary every two or three days. Do each section for two or three days.

Other good sections to study are words that begin GU, WH, QU, GE, GI, CE, CI, KA, KO and KU.

That is   **Dictionary Research.**

Celebrate finishing Chapter 6 by reading any or all of the following books.

Where The Wild Things Are   Maurice Sendak
Which Witch is Which?   Judi Barrett, Sharleen Collicott
Earthquack!   Margie Palatini, Barry Moser
A Story for Bear   Dennis Haseley, Jim LaMarche
My Storybook Dictionary   (Groller Incorporated, Danbury, CT)

Wall

Quack

Umbrella

An "active" Learner…

wants the right answer,

wants to know what makes the right answer "right",

wants to know how their wrong answers are wrong,

thinks about why we do it that way,

wonders and thinks about better ways to do it,

imagines that they will do what they can not do yet,

expects that they will learn what they try to learn,

expects to be wrong a lot when they start to learn something new,

finds and enjoys the time it takes to learn,

remembers when they did not know what they know now,

does not put down others for what they do not know yet,

expects to make mistakes, to enjoy them, and to learn from them,

is not in a hurry to laugh at other's mistakes (laughs with others, not at them!),

is the first, or at least the second, to see their own mistakes,

likes to focus on a problem, likes to think a long time about something hard,

studies how good teachers teach, what good teachers do that helps learners,

likes to help others learn, and likes to learn with others,

likes to share what they learn, with those who want to hear it,

talks about what they learn with friends, parents and grandparents,

asks parents and grandparents about what growing up was like for them,

asks parents and grandparents about what new things they are learning now,

checks their own work, sets their own goals, makes up their own problems to do,

thinks before they act, never needs to hear the rules, has already thought of them,

expects that they are not perfect, and does not expect others to be perfect.

-Dr. Hank

An Afterword

You have learned to read all of Volume 2, Book 1.

Reading Book 1 again should help you re-learn some things you may have forgotten by the end of Book 1, or may not have fully understood the first time you read Book 1.

Since you will already know how to read all the words, you will read faster this time.

Perhaps you can now read the Reader Script on some pages alone.

You can re-read any or all of the following for extra practice:

all the stories and sentences,

all the Words Lists,

all the pages that were hard for you the first time,

all the pages that had blanks for you to write in,

all the word families, sentences and stories you wrote in your Notebook,

the 2 chapters that were hardest for you,

all your favorite Celebration Books.

The extra practice with reading familiar words will be a good way, at this point in your learning progress, for you to get faster, more confident, and more comfortable at reading familiar words.

Learning Volume 2, Book 2 will be easier if you can read Volume 2, Book 1 very well.

Enjoy your new skill! Reading interesting books you could not read before is a good way to celebrate learning to read Book 1! Take time to enjoy your new skill before beginning Book 2.

APPENDIX 1:

TO THE LEARNER

The Suggested Words Lists Practice Plans, Games, Practice Calendar, and any directions of any other kind found in the text of any page in the book, **are all optional!**

This is a tool for you to use. It is your tool!

Learn to use it in the way that it most helps you to Learn.

You choose, with your Reader's help, the game or Practice Plan you use to practice a page.

Make up your own way to practice any page, or a way you've practiced at school.

Use ways to practice that are fun for you, so you will enjoy practicing a lot.

Use ways to practice that you and your Reader can see really help you to learn.

Have you ever climbed in the collection of connected bars that is called by two names on playgrounds, a "Jungle Gym" or "Monkey Bars?" It is a fun tool for getting better at climbing. It gives you a place where you can practice climbing a lot of different ways, using all your different muscles.

Use this Volume as a "Jungle Gym" that helps you practice reading, spelling, writing and storytelling!

With each section of Words Lists, sentences or stories you and your Reader practice:

you decide whether you, your Reader, or both of you read it first,

you decide how many times in a row to read it, and who reads each time,

you decide if you want to review an earlier page about the same subject first,

you decide if you want to look at the answer page before doing problems on this page,

you decide if you want to save some part of the page to do another day,

you decide if you want to think of your own way to practice any section.

And most important of all:

Have Fun Climbing!!

APPENDIX 2:

SOME FREE ADVICE FOR READERS

How to better assist your Learner while using this tool.

Letters @ Work has 3 Volumes.

Volume 2 has separate goals from Volumes 1 and 3.

Volume 1 developed the Learner's confidence by focusing on consistent letter-sound equivalencies.

The goals of **Volume 2: Consonants' Teams** are:

Learn to recognize and read teams of letters that work together to spell consonant sounds.

Learn the <u>different</u> letters and letter teams that can spell each consonant sound.

Practice some of the ways that Readers know <u>which</u> sound a team is spelling.

Learn to use the "sense" of a sentence to help you read some words' sounds.

Meet and practice <u>almost</u> all the ways to spell all the consonant sounds.

Meet and use verbs, nouns, adjectives and articles in noun phrases and verb phrases.

Volume 2 is split into Book One and Book Two to minimize wear and tear from repeated use.

Book One introduces the above subjects one at a time, each in isolation, for simplicity and clarity as the Learner first meets them. Much is left unsaid about each concept introduced. A "vowel sounds symbol system" is sometimes used to introduce examples where one vowel spells several different vowel sounds.

Book Two reviews each subject more systematically, with more detail, and begins to connect the subjects throughout the review process by using "the 3 laws of spelling" and "the 5 WH questions" as focusing lenses/tools. Book Two ends with a collection of Math Stories.

The goals of **Volume 3: Vowels' Teams** are:

Learn to recognize and read teams of letters that work together to spell vowel sounds.

Learn the different letters and letter teams that can spell each vowel sound.

Practice some of the ways that Readers know which sound a team is spelling.

Learn to use the "sense" of a sentence to help you read some words' sounds.

Meet and practice almost all the ways to spell all the vowel sounds.

Meet and use varied sentence constructions and extended word families.

Volume 2 uses the confident certainty with the letter sound identities of Volume 1 as a starting point and foundation to practice using more difficult letters, letter teams, grammar and context.

We hope the following comments will prove useful to the Reader.

When the material on a page is new, Learners will find value in repeating the page.

If the page was especially hard to do, it often helps to repeat the page immediately, when the answers the Learner struggled to reach are still fresh in memory. The immediate repetition will assist memorization, understanding and confidence.

With activities that were new or hard at first, but seemed easy at the end, two other strategies are useful. One is to repeat the page a day or two later. A second, which will work for some activities, is to repeat the activity with different examples from another page.

Independently repeating any pages a Learner has mastered is always useful.

Some activities that prove difficult at first, may be easier after doing subsequent pages. Likewise, looking at an "answer page" before doing a "problem page" will sometimes be helpful.

Many children express their interest in learning to read by pretending to do so.

Copying stories is a way children pretend to write. Writing a story as a child tells it, or a continuation of a story they have copied or read, and then giving them their words that you wrote for them to copy themselves, is a motivating confidence booster for many beginning readers. So is simply copying a story they like out of a book.

When writing on any page of Volume 2, write lightly in pencil, so that it can be completely erased. This allows future re-use of the page by the Learner, or future Learners who may use the book. Vowel sound color-coding ("colorizing") can be easily "erased" by using scissors to customize the size of self-stick file folder labels easily found for a dollar or so in any stationary store.

Preferable to "erasing" is to prep the page beforehand with blank file folder labels. Colorize the blank labels already on the page. Check your work. Keep the labels on for however long you like. Then remove them when you are done. By putting the labels back onto the contact sheet they originally came on, you will be able to reuse many of the same labels on future pages.

Prepping the labels beforehand requires a bit of extra work to begin with. But it does allow you to reuse many of the labels. It also keeps the pages beneath the labels blank for your eventual goal of reading the same examples without sound symbols, or for anyone else you may some day want to invite to use your copy of the book.

There are not many pages that invite you to colorize, and cutting the labels to place them above words is not difficult.

When a question in the Reader Script is followed by a long space and then the answer to the question, the long space invites the Reader to wait for the Learner to ponder the question. Practice with the process of pondering is often more valuable, in the long run, than hearing an immediate answer. With some questions herein, the "answer" to the question is not nearly as instructive as the questions the Learner generates in pursuit of the original question's answer, and the process of wrestling with them. Examples can be found at the bottom of pages 50, 64, 106, 128 and 143. Similarly, questions at the bottom of pages 102, 130 and 161 are useful with other pages as well.

All "colorizing" activities are examples of both the above types of question. Such questions can have value even when the final "answer" is pursued but not reached.

It is in the process of asking and answering their own questions that children practice independent thinking and learning skills. In the end, even hearing the answer will mean much more to them if they hear it after first wrestling with the details in search of their own answer.

But the above is only true if the information a Reader's question invites them to wrestle with is sufficiently plentiful and organized to clearly illustrate a pattern. The Words Lists in this book are organized to promote practice in observing patterns of sound-symbol relationships.

Remember that answers don't necessarily need to be arrived at immediately. Innumerable artists, inventors and scientists over the centuries have emphasized that solutions to their most difficult problems often arrived later, when thinking about other things, daydreaming or sleeping.

The Reader has an opportunity to help Learners see patterns, figure out relationships, and develop confidence in their ability to think for themselves. Here are some ways to help.

Increase the number of examples available

- Write additional words or sentences that are examples of the idea being focused on.

- Invite the Learner to dictate added words or sentences that the Reader types as the Learner speaks.

- Take turns saying additional words or sentences that are examples of the idea.

- Stories used as examples can be continued by the Reader, Learner, or both, to give more examples

- Model noticing out loud when examples of the "rule" or pattern occur while reading other books.

- Learner's questions can be answered by offering suitable examples rather than an answer.

- Invite comparisons of uncomplicated, similar examples where patterns can be quickly, easily seen.

- When a very organized section of Words Lists is completed, do it again skipping around randomly.

Build Learner confidence

- When a very organized section of Words Lists is completed, do it again skipping around randomly.

- Invite comparisons of uncomplicated, similar examples where patterns can be quickly, easily seen.

- Allow Learner to choose who reads each section of Learner Script first.

- If a paired-page activity is a difficult struggle, read the "answer" page first instead of second.

- Quickly reread any section you just finished before moving on.

- Repeat difficult sections several times, each time trying to "beat" time of prior reading.

- Keep the focus on the one idea while comparing consecutive examples that illustrate that idea.

- Take turns giving additional examples that illustrate the idea being focused on.

There are times when each of the above adjustments is especially useful, and times when each may be counterproductive. In choosing those times, the following anecdote is instructive.

Mary, a very bright and exceptionally self-motivated Hmong 2nd grader in an English-only classroom with a scripted curriculum the teacher was forbidden to adjust, was doing a worksheet with which she was not sufficiently prepared to succeed.

After Mary failed to understand the task working with the whole class, her teacher was able to make time to do the 10 problem worksheet one-on-one, explaining each example as the teacher did the first 5 problems without Mary understanding how or why the task was being done.

Mary began to get the idea with problems 6 & 7, and was able to do 8 thru 10 herself.

Many would regard this as a successful lesson. Mary was able to do at the end of the worksheet what she had been unable to do at the beginning of the worksheet.

Let's reconsider Mary's experience.

For 50% of the problems, Mary's feelings were "this is hard," "I can't do this," "some kids can but I can't." Frustration, futility and self-doubt invited surrender and distraction. Then for 20%

of the problems there was a bit of a glimmer mixed with those same negative feelings.

Then for 3 problems Mary was able to do the problems herself, though still struggling and uncertain whether she was doing it, and perhaps only understanding "how," but not "why."

While it seems to have been 70% painfully frustrating and 30% positive, reflect on the fact that each of the first 7 problems took 3 to 5 times as long to do as the last 3 took; which changes the ratio of time spent feeling futility or success from 70/30 to 90/10. Add the time spent trying throughout the whole-class lesson beforehand and the ratio is now 95/5.

Then consider the effect on a child not as exceptionally bright, persistent and self-motivated as Mary, who showed up after school for an extra 2 hours of tutoring 3-4 days a week for 6 months on a strictly voluntary basis without external rewards when she was free to be outside playing with friends each afternoon. Mary led her friends to tutoring instead.

In fact, Mary left the lesson eager to forget the whole experience as soon as possible.

Use adjustments that teach "I can," and sidestep long periods of time feeling "I can't."

For reasons expressed throughout Appendices 2 and 3, and others, these Volumes teach via many successive examples carefully structured to clearly illustrate spelling and grammar patterns. Explicit explanations aim to clarify and help focus the examples.

The examples consist of Words Lists, lists of sentences and some (very) short stories.

The sentences and stories are vehicles that provide examples. The twin purposes, to (1) illustrate a current "lesson," and (2) practice "recent lessons," wrote every story herein. Whatever came to mind that best served those two purposes, within the limits of what letters and sounds had already been introduced by that point in the book, was used. Inevitably, some author views and values, "biases" for those who prefer the word, were engaged in this process.

Stories express values, lessons, viewpoints. Choosing your child's values is not our purpose. We trust Readers will find opportunities to share your family's values as you work and read together.

APPENDIX 3:

LEARN TO LEARN

We are defining a second goal to assist and improve the Learner's pursuit of our first goal (the first goal is learning how to read and spell). Our second goal is that the Learner will learn to learn.

Young people learn abstract "rules" and "principles" by seeing (and holding in hand) repeated examples of the rule or principle in action, and only then are they able to comprehend and apply the rule or principle, and also describe it **if** given the language **after** they learn to use and recognize the principle. But they learn to recognize the principle by seeing, holding and/or using many consecutive, well-organized occurrences of the principle in action.

Young children need to see, feel and use many specific, preferably organized, examples of a rule before a spoken general statement of that rule will evoke those examples in the child's mind!

Adults helping children to learn often start with a general explanation of a rule or principle, expecting children to visualize specific examples from a description of a general rule. Young children won't visualize the example from hearing the explanation until enough **uninterrupted, organized, specific, individual examples** are experienced. This book tries to provide long lists of effectively organized examples that illustrate the ways letters spell words and the ways words work together in sentences to make sense.

It is not necessary to answer every question "now!"

There is long-term value in admiring a Learner's question, and then admiring their thoughts as they think of and mention them. Let the child's thoughtful interaction with the organization of the information function at its own pace, and focus on getting the child to interact thoughtfully with the information. Do not be in a hurry to put the words to the right answer in the child's mouth. Instead, listen to the pace and process of the child's learning, and learn, by listening, to better help the child focus and practice their thinking.

This very important strategy requires noteworthy patience from adults. Young children do not "answer" questions fast enough for adults, so adults supply the answers when the young child has barely begun to process the question at their speed, a speed too slow for an adult to see. Thus, adults normally preclude a child's "thinking practice" with the adult's hurry to get to the "answer" faster, and falsely judge the child's ability to re-state the words to the answer, as stated by the adult, as an understanding of the principle. Meanwhile, the child remains unable to employ the principle, despite saying the words.

Give your Learner room to practice wondering at and thinking about a question at their own pace, a little bit here and now, a little bit more later. Once the child proves able to employ a principle, the words that state the principle can have real functional meaning.

We are not suggesting you never answer a question the Learner asks. We are suggesting you do some of both, answer some questions, let them think about other questions. Choose which questions it's best to answer and which it's best to let them wrestle with thinking about on their own as they practice the organized examples that prompted them to ask the question, and any other examples that seem to apply.

Be willing to respond to a Learner's question by saying,

    1. "That's a good question to think about,"

    2. "Let's keep that question in mind while we practice,"

or 3. "See if you get any ideas about that as we practice."

Or, if the Learner seems ready to work out the answer to their question now, and you want to help them do so, offer a list of additional examples (of your own or from another page in this book) that will focus the Learner's attention on data that will help the Learner answer the question.

Invite the Learner to study those examples and tell you the answer when they see it.

Our aim in Volume 2 is to prepare not only the Learner's knowledge and use of letter-sound identities and their confidence in their own ability to learn to read, but also the **specific, active learning skills** that will best assist their tackling Volume 3 more confidently and successfully, and **every future learning challenge they experience.**

We believe that Learners ultimately reach **long range goals** quicker if they develop the **habit** of looking for answers in the information itself, asking and seeking answers to their own questions. Try to develop in them a habit of belief, an <u>expectation based on their experiences</u> with you, that they **CAN ask useful questions and CAN think productively about the answers to their questions**, independently, by studying information thoughtfully, and not only by being told the answer. If you can build a fun, confident habit of enjoying actively thinking about the information in front of them, they will gradually begin to learn more quickly as they get more confident and active about having questions and thinking about their questions.

And then do not expect too much of first answers, or lead them to expect immediate answers.

Help them have a relaxed habit of wondering at a question a while. When they share an idea, compliment the idea **without telling them it was right or wrong**. Ask them if they can think of any ways to decide when their idea is true and when it isn't.

Let them wonder without interference, impatience or stress about how quick or how right an answer is. Give them stress-free time to practice the enjoyment of thinking about the answer to their question at their own speed for their own fun in doing so.

In the long run, you speed the ability for answers to arrive more quickly if you build the Learner's belief that **they are the Active Center of that process!**

We recommend a similar policy with regard to mistakes the Learner makes while reading. Sometimes, just say the word correctly. Sometimes, wait and see how soon a child catches their own mistake, then compliment their thinking or their effort to notice their own mistakes, rather than their answer.

Sometimes, respond to a misread letter (that the child has read successfully in the past) by having them read many words in a row that use the letter they misread, without first pointing out their error, until the evidence of the other words shows it to them.

The Reader can also help the Learner by reminding the Learner of the things the Learner is trying to keep in mind as they practice. The Reader can help the Learner remember the following:

- Know your goals at each practice.

- Think about your goals as you practice; keep in mind what you are trying to learn.

- Point to and read each word in the Reader Script with me as I read that word to you.

- Try your own Practice Plans from time to time, and decide whether you like them.

- When you first learn to read or spell a letter, that is the most important time to practice it a lot!

- As you learn each new letter, **use it**, write words and sentences with it, practice reading it **now**!

The Reader can help the Learner learn to learn by asking the following questions, every page:

Which page do you want to do next?

Which Practice Plan do you want to use for this page this time?

Appendix 4:

Celebration Books for Book One

A brief note regarding the Celebration books recommended at the end of each Chapter.

While these books are organized by Chapter, any of them can usefully celebrate any Chapter. For best effect, read the books you choose to read repeatedly over the course of several weeks. Repetitive practice with familiar books works as incentive, reward and exercise for emerging skills.

If you can't find a given book in your public library, try the school library. Teachers and school librarians will gladly help parents or siblings who are making an extra effort to read with children. Some used book stores have excellent selections also, and more affordable prices.

You may find it useful to add other books recommended by teachers or parents on these pages.

Book Title	Author, Illustrator

CHAPTER 1

The Name Jar	Yangsook Choi
Once Upon a Time	Niki Daly
Once Upon a Time	Vivian French, John Prater
Inside, Outside, Upside Down	Stan and Jan Barenstain
The Cat in the Hat Beginner Book Dictionary	Dr. Seuss and P. D. Eastman

CHAPTER 2

The Red Tree	Shaun Tan
Where's Pup	Dayle Ann Dodds, Pierre Pratt
I am a little giraffe.	Francois Crozat
I Read Signs	Tara Hoban
Milet Picture Dictionary: English and others*	Sadat Turhan and others, Sally Hagin

*(13 editions…1 English only, 12 bilingual editions: English and Albanian, Arabic, Bengali, Chinese, French, German, Italian, Somali, Spanish, Turkish, Urdu, Vietnamese)

We recommend looking at what all the alphabets and languages look like. Enjoy looking and comparing. If one of these is your native language, and English a 2nd language, read the book using both languages.

CHAPTER 3

Ruby's Wish	Shirin Yin Bridges, Sophie Blackall
Little Buggy	Kevin O'Malley
Amazing Grace	Mary Hoffman, Caroline Birch
A Fly Went By	Mike and Marshall McClintock
Little Rabbit's First Word Book Ever	Alan Baker

CHAPTER 4

Night Cat	Margaret Beames, Sue Hitchcock
Duck in the Truck	Jez Alborough
Bad Boys	Margie Palatini, Henry Cole
Courage	Bernard Waber
Richard Scarry's Best Word Book Ever	Richard Scarry

CHAPTER 5

I Stink	Kate and Jim McMullan
My Brother, Ant	Betsy Byars
Everett Anderson's 1-2-3	Lucille Clifton, Ann Grifalconi
Babies On the Go	Linda Ashman, Jane Dyer
One Grain of Sand: A Lullaby	Pete Seeger, Linda Wingerter

CHAPTER 6

Where The Wild Things Are	Maurice Sendak
Which Witch is Which?	Judi Barrett, Sharleen Collicott
Earthquack!	Margie Palatini, Barry Moser
A Story for Bear	Dennis Haseley, Jim LaMarche
My Storybook Dictionary	(Groller Incorporated, Danbury, CT)

APPENDIX 5:

SOME ANSWERS FOR BOOK ONE

Page 85

happy	grumpy	silly	funny	merry	angry	messy
happier ✓	grumpier ✓	sillier ✓	funnier ✓	merrier ✓	angrier ✓	messier ✓
happi<u>est</u>	grumpi<u>est</u>	silli<u>est</u>	funni<u>est</u>	merri<u>est</u>	angri<u>est</u>	messi<u>est</u>

empty	sunny	foggy	yummy	fancy	dingy	dusty
emptier ✓	sunnier ✓	foggier ✓	yummier ✓	fancier ✓	dingier ✓	dustier ✓
empti<u>est</u>	sunni<u>est</u>	foggi<u>est</u>	yummi<u>est</u>	fanci<u>est</u>	dingi<u>est</u>	dusti<u>est</u>

Page 103

Jim swim_**s**_ when Jim can swim.

That dog wag_**s**_ his tail if he is happy.

Wally will wax his floor after he mop_**s**_ it.

Walter wait_**s**_ every day for the bus.

Georgia give_**s**_ away the funniest wax wigs at the mall.

That dragon swim_**s**_ on Saturdays, too.

Page 105

Some birds <u>swim</u>. The dogs <u>jump</u>. Cats <u>purr</u>. Whistlers <u>whistle</u>. Even little frogs <u>jump</u>.

What bird swim<u>s</u>? The dog jump<u>s</u>. My cat purr<u>s</u>. Which whistle whistle<u>s</u>? My frog jump<u>s</u>.

Many things <u>sing</u>.   Many bees <u>sting</u>.   Many singers <u>sing</u>.

I <u>wonder</u>.   You <u>help</u>.   We <u>floss</u>.   They <u>giggle</u>.   Marc and Mark <u>run</u> more than I do.

That thing sing<u>s</u>.   One bee sting<u>s</u>.   One singer sing<u>s</u>   Who sing<u>s</u> lullabies?

She swim<u>s</u> every morning and he swim<u>s</u> every evening.   Who swim<u>s</u> here daily?

Jessica spell<u>s</u> well.   Sandy stud<u>ies</u> spelling.   Martin say<u>s</u> Cecilia swim<u>s</u> faster than Mary.

You could be help<u>ing</u>.   I would be danc<u>ing</u>.   We should be work<u>ing</u>.

I am help<u>ing</u>. We are danc<u>ing</u>. She is work<u>ing</u>. He was work<u>ing</u> when we were work<u>ing</u>.

We hate sit<u>ting</u> still.   He likes talk<u>ing</u>.   They liked walk<u>ing</u>. We talk about walk<u>ing</u> too.

Last week I walk<u>ed</u>. We talk<u>ed</u> last month. She s<u>a</u>ng at a concert last year.

Yesterday I sw<u>a</u>m in a river. Yesterday my sister sw<u>a</u>m, then she fish<u>ed</u> in a lake.

The banjo player play<u>ed</u> for an hour, two hours ago. A drummer r<u>a</u>ng bells with sticks.

Page 121

strum	drip	spot	scan	rub	sled
strums	drips	spots	scans	rubs	sleds
strumming	dripping	spotting	scanning	rubbing	sledding
strummed	dripped	spotted	scanned	rubbed	sledded

stroke	skate	tame	mine	bake	move	close
strokes	skates	tames	mines	bakes	moves	closes
stroking	skating	taming	mining	baking	moving	closing
stroked	skated	tamed	mined	baked	moved	closed

stride	ride	skim	can	bat	kick	clip
strides	rides	skims	cans	bats	kicks	clips
striding	riding	skimming	canning	batting	kicking	clipping
strode	rode	skimmed	canned	batted	kicked	clipped

rude	late	tame	dim	hot	stiff	dull
ruder	later	tamer	dimmer	hotter	stiffer	duller
rudest	latest	tamest	dimmest	hottest	stiffest	dullest

nice	thick	fake	huge	big	quick	sad
nicer	thicker	faker	huger	bigger	quicker	sadder
nicest	thickest	fakest	hugest	biggest	quickest	saddest

Page 129

hazy	furry	tidy	wormy	hungry
hazier	furrier	tidier	wormier	hungrier
haziest	furriest	tidiest	wormiest	hungriest

Appendix 6:

Colorized Answers for Book One

Tools we Colorize pages with are Crayola Markers, Rose Art Pencils, and an ordinary wooden #2 pencil.

The Vowel Sound Symbols are:

Short Vowels (Rose Art Pencils = **R.A.P.**)   &   Long Vowels (Crayola Markers = **C.M.**)

Orange	circle	a	Red	circle
Yellow Green	"	e	Green	"
Yellow	"	i	Yellow (+red)**	"
Orchid	"	o	Violet (purple)	"
Sky Blue	circle	u	Blue	"U"

((** = red pencil "pupil" (dot) in a yellow marker "eye" (circle)))

Other Vowel Sounds

Schwa = Pencil * period (dot)   OO = Blue C.M. "O"

Silent **E** = Pencil * minus sign (dash)   OI, OY = Gray C.M. "O"

ULL = Pencil * "O"   AU, AW, ALL = Brown R.A.P. circle   OU, OW = Brown C.M. "O"

OR = Brown R.A.P. "x"   AR = Orchid R.A.P. "x"   AIR, ERE = Red R.A.P. "x"

((*=ordinary #2 lead-in-wood pencil))

Those are all of our Tools and Symbols for colorizing Sound Symbols.

("Colorizing" is not really a word. We made it up to refer to our Sound Symbol colors.)

Conserve these colors by using them only for Sound Symbol Colorizing.

Keep them in a box separate from the other Markers & Pencils that came in the same package.

Use other colors of Markers & Pencils for illustrations and art. Use colorizing tools only for colorizing.

at	ate	bet	beat	bit	bite	hop	hope	cut	cute
scat	skate	said	seed	sit	sight	rod	road	cub	cube
ran	rain	read	read	it	eye	want	toe	up	few

turn	skate	pull
work	hope	full
girl	cute	helpful

who	toy	saw	how
two	boil	pause	loud
you	boy	all	now

four	are	their
for	far	there
before	start	pair

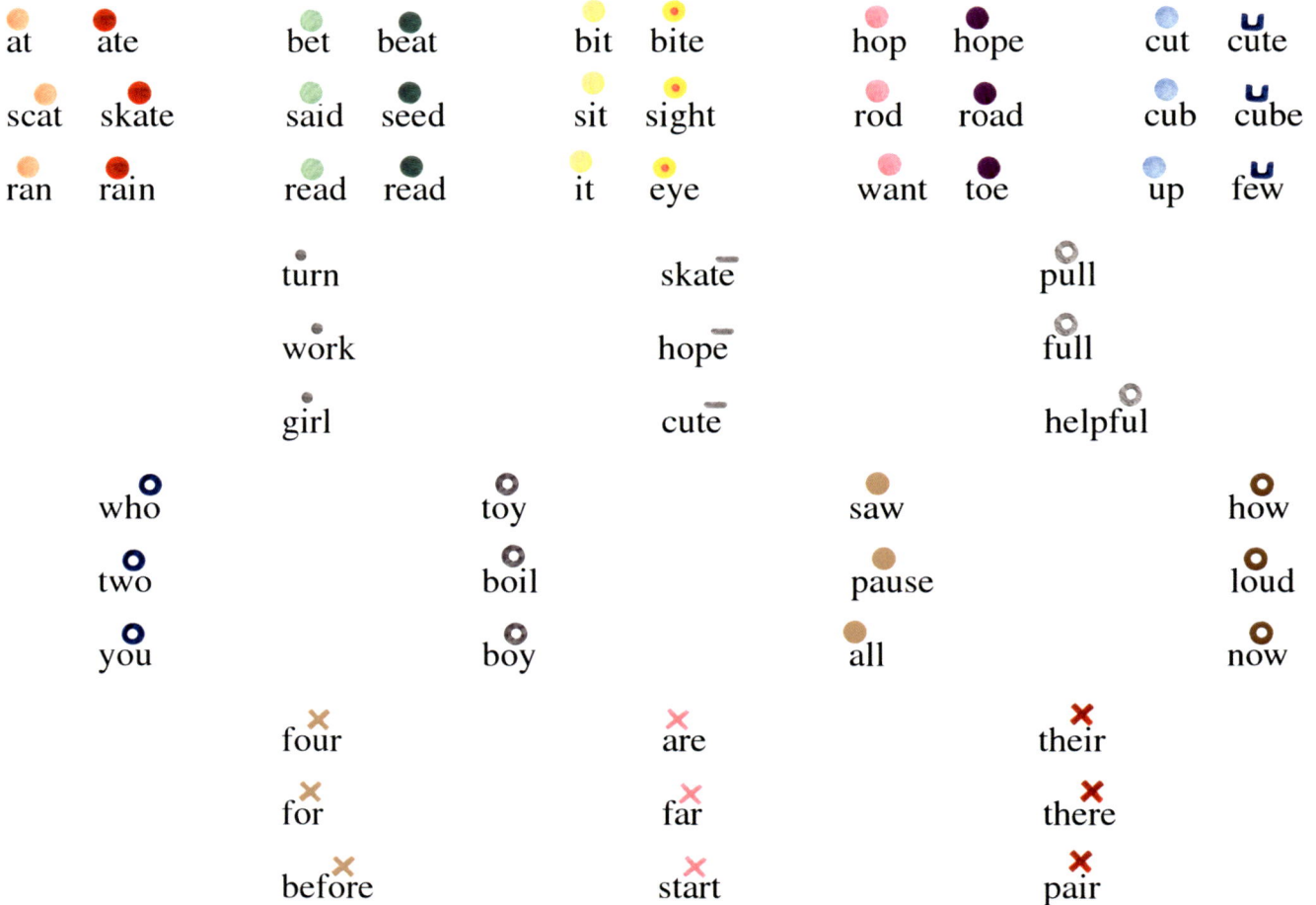

Pronunciation of vowel sounds is different from section to section of the USA.

In a few places it differs from county to county.
Even dictionaries disagree about some pronunciations.

When the author researched whether the first E in emergency was a schwa or short E sound,

one dictionary said it was E's name sound and another said it was a short I sound.
For some syllables most dictionaries list 2 sounds, either of which is "right." (See "long," "loss.")
Language is for speaking with and understanding the people around you.
The way your family and neighbors pronounce a word is the right way for you to pronounce it.
In coding the vowel sounds in this Appendix, we have used dictionaries.
When dictionaries offer 2 different vowel sounds, we picked one, but both are "correct."

The O in many words gets a short U in some dictionaries and a schwa in other dictionaries.
The point of saying all this is just this...

If you chose a short U sound, & we have given it a schwa sound, that doesn't mean you are wrong.

If you have a schwa sound, & we have U's short sound symbol, that doesn't mean you are wrong.
Use this Appendix as an easy way to check your choices of vowel sounds.
But when your choice and ours disagree, the only important thing is

whether the people around you understand what word you are saying when you say it.

This Appendix contains all the Words Lists and Sentences the main text invites you to colorize.

Compare your use of our Vowel Sound Symbols to a page in this Appendix to correct your work.

Page 24

we	we	they	they	my	you	all	say
he	was	day	the	by	do	ball	says
she	what	today	then	try	to	tall	saying
me	when	stay	than	fly	too	small	said
be	went	play	this	dry	two	wall	
bee	will	players	that	sky	of		
see	were	ways	with		from	your	or

pump	sing	see	sink	think	bring	buy	sit
pumps	sings	sees	sinks	thinks	brings	buys	sits
pumping	singing	seeing	sinking	thinking	bringing	buying	sitting
pumped	sang	saw	sank	thought	brought	bought	sat

fast	big	small	thin	thick	low	slow
faster	bigger	smaller	thinner	thicker	lower	slower
fastest	biggest	smallest	thinnest	thickest	lowest	slowest

Page 25

They play ball on Saturday, on the thick grass of a soccer field.

The smaller soccer players seem to run and turn faster than most of the taller players do.

We play handball all day every day, hitting the small ball against the tall wall.

They play soccer Thursdays and Saturdays , if they see that the sky is dry.

We saw that singer singing in a play last Saturday, a play with a lot of singing.

We sat on the small wall under the tall hill thinking of ways to play and stay dry.

We had to play inside today, to stay dry all day long.

Page 27

give	live	life	wife	hive	dive
gives	lives	lives	wives	hives	dives
giving	living	gift	jive	dive	diving
gave	lived	gifts		dives	dove

have	half	calf	brave	pave	save
has	halves	calves	braves	paves	saves
having			braving	paving	saving
had			braved	paved	saved

Page 28

We <u>strove</u> to <u>move</u> <u>clover</u> from the grove over the river, to <u>move</u> the <u>clover</u> by the <u>cloves</u>.

We put our <u>gloves</u> on, put the <u>clover</u> on trucks, and the <u>drivers</u> <u>drove</u> the trucks.

The <u>drivers</u> <u>drove</u> the trucks full of <u>clover</u> over the river, where we <u>removed</u> the <u>clover</u>.

We had our <u>gloves</u> on to <u>remove</u> the <u>clover</u> from the trucks that <u>drove</u> it over the river.

We <u>removed</u> the <u>clover</u> from the backs of the trucks that <u>drove</u> the <u>clover</u> over the river.

As we put the <u>clover</u> in stacks by the <u>cloves</u>, our stacks <u>improved</u>, they got a bit better.

Page 40

drizzle

jazz

guzzle

fizzes

zen

jog

jam

jump

just

jingle

germs

gentle

urgent

gender

gerbil

gist

magic

urging

gym

energy

judge

lodge

pledge

giggle

tingle

fix

fizz

fall

flex

fins

self

surf

sniff

sniffles

soft

life

safe

strife

sofa

wife

van

vigor

ever

never

serve

give

live

strive

drive

dive

gave

have

half

wave

paved

move

remove

prove

disprove

approve

improve

love

gloves

oven

cover

over

stove

seven

eleven

given

gravel

level

pivot

driver

river

liver

favor

flavor

lever

move

moves

moving

moved

love

loves

loving

loved

drive

drives

driving

drove

give

gives

giving

gave

have

has

having

had

see

sees

seeing

saw

say

says

saying

said

do

does

doing

did

age 42

zero   one   two   three   four   five   six   seven   eight   nine   ten   eleven   twelve

Page 70

you	yap	gypsy	beyond	very	valley	apply	try	my
yet	yip	mystery	mayor	city	volley	supply	cry	by
Yeti	yum	byte	crayon	silly	pulley	petrify	fry	why

Page 73

yip	yap	yell	dance	prance	fence	mince	gyp
yips	yaps	yells	dances	prances	fences	minces	gyps
yipping	yapping	yelling	dancing	prancing	fencing	mincing	gypping
yipped	yapped	yelled	danced	pranced	fenced	minced	gypped

urge	bulge	judge	edge	bridge	verge	merge	rhyme
urges	bulges	judges	edges	bridges	verges	merges	rhymes
urging	bulging	judging	edging	bridging	verging	merging	rhyming
urged	bulged	judged	edged	bridged	verged	merged	rhymed

yam	yell	byte	mystic	key	monkey	money	rhyme	fly
yams	yells	bytes	mystics	keys	monkeys	monies	rhymes	flies

yip	yap	mystery	valley	volley	pulley	city	cry	try
yips	yaps	mysteries	valleys	volleys	pulleys	cities	cries	tries

dance	fence	berry	trance	pencil	recess	accident	judge	bridge
dances	fences	berries	trances	pencils	recesses	accidents	judges	bridges

Page 123

When <u>Dave</u> and I <u>drive</u> up to a house, pull to a stop, and park, we always hear the kids who <u>live</u> there yelling, "Here are the <u>movers</u>."

And <u>Dave</u> always says, "They're the ones <u>moving</u>, not me. I'm <u>living</u> in the same house I <u>lived</u> in when I was a kid, the same house my dad built."

<u>Dave</u> <u>loves</u> to tell the kids that they are the <u>movers</u>, not <u>Dave</u> and I. But the kids call us the <u>movers</u> anyway. Some kids call us home <u>movers</u>, but we don't <u>move</u> homes or houses, we <u>move</u> <u>everything</u> that people keep in them.

We put our <u>gloves</u> on and put the people's belongings in the back of our big truck.

We start with the big, <u>heavy</u> things, like <u>ovens</u>, <u>stoves</u>, dishwashers and cabinets.

Then we <u>cover</u> <u>everything</u> with thick, soft <u>covers</u>.

Then we add lots of smaller, <u>heavy</u> things, like boxes of books, dishes or tools.

We <u>shove</u> <u>everything</u> as close together as we can get it, so it can't <u>move</u> or slide in the back of the truck later, when we <u>drive</u> the truck. If there is no space between things, the things <u>have</u> no room to <u>move</u> around and bump into each other. If nothing can <u>move</u> or bump, nothing can break. We hope. We <u>cover</u> <u>everything</u> with soft cloth just in case.

drive	live	love	move	have	shove	cover
drives	lives	loves	moves	has	shoves	covers
driving	living	loving	moving	having	shoving	covering
drove	lived	loved	moved	had	shoved	covered

Page 163

wag   Wes   wall   well   wig

wags   wet   walls   welt   wit

wax   wed   Walt   weld   wilt

waxes   wets   Walt's   welds   will

waxing   weds   Walter   welts   willing

was   won   wonder   wonders   wondering   wondered

what   one   ones   once   one's

wan   want   wad   waddle   waffle

wants   wads   waddles   waffles

wanting   waddling

wanted   waddled

wag   wags   wax   waxes   waxing   waft   wafting

wall   walls   Walt   Walt's   Walter   Walter's

war   warn   warm   warmer   warmest   warming   warning

wit   wig   will   wilt   win   wick   wing

wiggle   winter   wind   twig   swig   swim   swift